# WORLD OF OUR FATHERS

The Jews of Eastern Europe

Also by MILTON MELTZER

REMEMBER THE DAYS
A Short History of the Jewish American

HUNTED LIKE A WOLF
The Story of the Seminole War

BOUND FOR THE RIO GRANDE
The Mexican Struggle, 1845–1850

SLAVERY
From the Rise of Western Civilization to Today (2 volumes)

A PICTORIAL HISTORY OF BLACKAMERICANS
(with Langston Hughes)

THE EYE OF CONSCIENCE
Photographers and Social Change

LANGSTON HUGHES
A Biography

UNDERGROUND MAN

THE RIGHT TO REMAIN SILENT

# WORLD OF OUR FATHERS

## The Jews of Eastern Europe

MILTON MELTZER

FARRAR, STRAUS AND GIROUX | NEW YORK

LIBRARY OF CONGRESS CATALOGING IN PUBLICATION DATA
Meltzer, Milton
  World of our fathers.

  1.  Jews in Eastern Europe—Juvenile literature.
[1.  Jews in Eastern Europe—History]  I.  Title.
DS135.E83M35  1974    914.7′06′924    74-14755
ISBN  0-374-38530-0

Acknowledgment is made for permission to quote from the
following works: A Dreamer's Journey by Morris R. Cohen,
Copyright 1949 by the Free Press; My Memoirs by I. L. Peretz,
Copyright © by Fred Goldberg 1964, by permission of Citadel
Press, Secaucus, N.J.; Morning Stars by Zalman Shazar, by per-
mission of The Jewish Publication Society of America; "The City
of Slaughter" by Chaim Nachman Bialik, translated by Joseph
Leftwich, by permission of Thomas Yoseloff, A. S. Barnes & Co.;
Life Is with People by Zborowski and Herzog, by permission of
International Universities Press, Inc.; Jewish Life in the Ukraine
by Michael Charnofsky, © 1965 by Michael Charnofsky, and
Tell the Children by Samuel Schwartz, © 1959 by Samuel
Schwartz, by permission of Exposition Press, Inc., Jericho, N.Y.;
Trial and Error by Chaim Weizmann, by permission of Harper &
Row, Inc.; "The Eastern European Era in Jewish History" by
Abraham Joshua Heschel, from Voices from the Yiddish, edited
by Howe and Greenberg, by permission of the University of
Michigan Press; Promised Land by Mary Antin, by permission of
Houghton Mifflin Company; My Life with the Microbes by
Selman Waksman, Copyright 1954 by Selman Waksman, M.D.,

*For my daughters,*
JANE *and* AMY

# CONTENTS

# Foreword

When I was growing up in Worcester, Massachusetts, I had little sense of being a Jew. We lived in a mixed neighborhood of three-decker houses. There were other Jewish families on Union Hill, but there were many more who were Irish, Polish, Lithuanian, Swedish, German, Italian, Armenian in origin. Some were Protestant, more were Catholic. We played prisoner's base together and king of the mountain, and baseball and football and hockey. And we went to the same school. Many of their parents, like mine, had come from Europe to the Promised Land, so most of us were the first generation to be born in America.

My mother and father had met in New York, after emigrating from Europe. All I knew about their origins was that both came from what was then Austro-Hungary. The old maps showed it to have been a large, pasted-together empire, of many nationalities. It sprawled over much of Eastern Europe. Just which part, which town or village they were born in, I never learned until long after childhood. (And discovered only recently that my impression had been wrong.) Not that it was a secret. My mother and father simply did not talk about their life in the old country. And all wrapped up in myself, I never thought to ask. They were here, in Worcester, this was now, and I had no time for anything else. The past didn't interest me then (who would have thought I'd write history one day?) and the future stretched only as far as tomorrow morning. My mother and father had had a little schooling in Europe, I knew, but nothing that prepared them for anything but unskilled labor. Both had worked in factories before coming to Worcester. Now my mother was staying at home to raise a family of three sons. And my father tried to support us by washing windows.

I remember that they spoke only English. It was no doubt a faulty and accented English. They rarely used Yiddish. That must have been because they wanted us to grow up "American." And the faster we learned the American language, the better.

My father was not a believer. He did not go to the synagogue on the other side of the hill. I vaguely remember going with my mother once or twice on a high holiday. Still, I was prepared briefly for a *bar mitzvah*, the ceremony for boys reaching the age of thirteen. But it only meant that for several months a bearded old man came to our house after I came home from school, hammered a bit of Hebrew into my reluctant ears, and listened to me memorizing a set speech. As soon as that Saturday's ordeal passed, the lessons ended. I think now I was put through it because my mother was concerned with what her mother and father might think (they lived in far-off New York) if we hadn't done it. By the time my younger brother reached thirteen, she didn't even bother.

There were no books about Jewish life or history in our house (or about any other subject, for that matter). And being Jewish was never discussed. Until, that is, a neighbor told my mother that I was seen "fooling around" with the daughter of an Irish cop on the next block. Then my mother let me know (with a slap in the face) that this was a bad thing. Jew and non-Jew couldn't mix. "It never works out." Later, in high school, I fell in love with a classmate who happened to be Protestant. But she lived far away on the other side of town and I never asked her to come to my home. I spent a lot of time in hers, but by then I was old enough to conceal it better, or perhaps my mother was too beset by the Depression, which had come on, to think this mattered much. It did matter, to me, but in the end we each fell in love with and married someone else.

I left Worcester to go to a college in New York. From then on, I was on my own. My father died when I was a student. He never talked to me about his childhood. I don't know if he ever would have, even if I'd had the sense to ask the right questions. He was a silent man. I loved him, although I cannot remember a single conversation between us. My mother was far more talkative. She probably would have told me much about life in the old country that I'd delight in knowing now. But I never showed any interest in it. And by the time I was smart enough to want to know, it was too late. She was ten years gone.

If my own parents told me nothing about my people's past, then surely my teachers might have taught me something about it. They didn't. I think the Worcester schools were good ones—at least I thrived in them—but they too, like my mother and father, were hell-bent on Americanizing us. The classrooms were full of first-generation Americans, and the teachers took it as their business to mold us into true-blue citizens, loyal, faithful, patriotic. The only language that mattered was English. The only culture we heard about was Anglo-Saxon. The only history to study was American. Oh, a bit of British history was wedged in to let us know what our country had broken away from, and later there was some ancient history, Greek and Roman. But little in between. And certainly nothing about those countries so many of us sitting on the hard benches could trace our roots to.

As I went from grade school to junior high and then high school, I noticed that the proportion of immigrant children gradually dropped. Many left school to go to work. There were several high schools in the town; one specialized in preparing the "better" students from all over the city for college. When I entered it, I discovered there were far more boys and girls with Anglo-Saxon names than in the school I had come from. Some of these were excellent students, others seemed to be there only because their parents had the money to assure a college education. They dressed differently, spoke differently, behaved differently. I wanted to look like them, talk like them, act like them. They had an ease and assurance I envied. I worked hard at my studies, joined school clubs, made new friends. But the only one of the strangers I grew close to was the girl I fell in love with. And I never really felt at ease in her home or with her family.

I had too little knowledge of my past to find it solid ground to stand on. Nor could I penetrate the strange world of my new classmates. Who was I? From what did I come? To what did I belong? Only now did these questions begin to trouble me. It took a very long time, seeking the answers, all the while trying, like most immigrants and their children, to follow the American command to rise and assimilate.

I've learned something at last about my family's past. Not just my mother's and father's, but the life of the Jews in Eastern Europe from whom most of today's 6 million American Jews sprang. It is a world almost unknown to most of us, the world of our grandparents and great-grandparents. Who were they? What color and tension did their lives have? What concerns and what hopes? Getting to know those people—the places they lived in, the work they did, the enemies they feared, the customs and habits and values they lived by—we begin to know ourselves.

# WORLD OF
# OUR FATHERS

The Jews of Eastern Europe

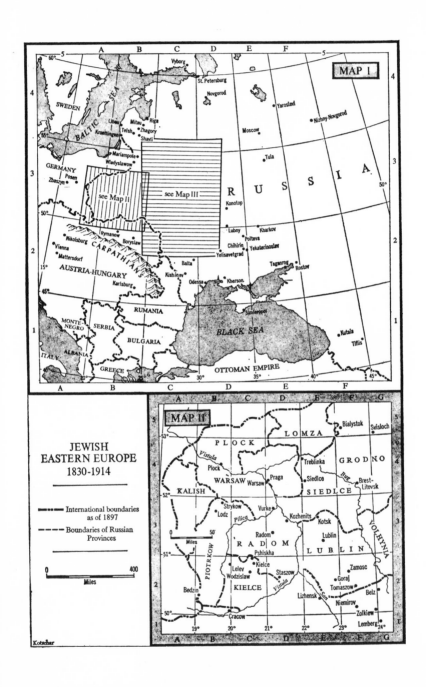

MAP 1

A B C D E F

Vyborg

St. Petersburg

Novgorod

SWEDEN

BALTIC SEA

Libau Riga
Mitau
Telsh Zhagory
Kroettingen Shavli

Mariampole

Wladyslawow

GERMANY

Posen

Zbaszyn

see Map II

see Map III

R U S S I A

Moscow

Yaroslavl

Nizhny-Novgorod

Tula

Konotop

CARPATHIANS

Rymanow
Borislaw

Nikolsburg

Vienna

Mattersdorf

AUSTRIA-HUNGARY

Karlsburg

Balta

Kishinev

Lubny

Chihirin

Yelisavetgrad

Kharkov

Poltava

Yekaterinoslav

Odessa

Kherson

Taganrog

Rostov

RUMANIA

MONTE-
NEGRO

SERBIA

BULGARIA

Simferopol

BLACK SEA

Kutais

Tiflis

ITALY

ALBANIA

GREECE

OTTOMAN EMPIRE

A B C D E F

JEWISH
EASTERN EUROPE
1830-1914

━━━ International boundaries
as of 1897

━ ━ Boundaries of Russian
Provinces

0          400
Miles

MAP II

A B C D E F G

Bialystok

Svisloch

PLOCK

LOMZA

Vistula

Plock

Treblinka

GRODNO

WARSAW

Warsaw Praga

Siedlce

Bug

Brest-
Litovsk

KALISH

SIEDLCE

Strykow

Lodz

Pilica

Vurke

Kozhenits

Kotsk

Lublin

VOLHYNIA

Radom

R A D O M

L U B L I N

Lelev

Wodzislaw

Kielce

Pshiskha

Staszow

Zamosc

Goraj

Tomaszow

PIOTRKOW

KIELCE

Vistula

Bedzin

Lizhensk

Niemirov

Belz

Cracow

Zolkiew

Lemberg

A B C D E F G

19° 20° 21° 22° 23° 24°

Kotschar

After the partitions of Poland (1772, 1793, and 1795), Eastern European Jews came under the rule of Russia, Austria, and Prussia. These maps locate many of the place names in *World of Our Fathers*

# 1 WHERE THEY CAME FROM

HALF THE JEWS OF THE WORLD LIVED IN
Eastern Europe in the year 1800.

That region isn't the Eastern Europe we identify
today as the Soviet Union and the Communist countries
west of it. In Jewish history, Eastern Europe was taken
as the area bounded by the Rhine River on the west and
the Dnieper on the east. Its northern extreme was the
Baltic and its southern, the Black Sea.

Compared with Western Europe, it was backward.
Its population was mostly peasants (many of them serfs
until the 1860's), with some artisans and workers.

The Jews of Eastern Europe were *Ashkenazi*, with
their own language, Yiddish. Over the centuries they had
developed a unique group life. Their number grew rapidly, from 1 million in 1775 to 5.5 million in 1875. In
1939, on the eve of Hitler's holocaust, there were 7
million Jews in Eastern Europe; millions of others born
there had gone to live abroad, the great majority in the
United States.

Where did the Eastern European Jews come from?
Why were so many living in this place, where legal and
economic barriers made life for the Jews so much worse
than elsewhere?

The true beginnings of Eastern European Jewry have

been clouded by myth and legend. It is known that there were Jewish settlements in Europe as far back as the time of the Second Temple (70 C.E.). But the centers of Jewish life were in Babylonia, Egypt, and Palestine. From the third to the tenth century, Babylonia was looked upon by Jews everywhere as their spiritual heart. Its large Jewish center developed a rich cultural life that helped maintain Jewish continuity in the *Diaspora*.

When the Moslem faith was carried abroad on Arab banners in the seventh century, Babylonian Jews migrated too. They settled in Palestine, North Africa, and several places in Western Europe. There is some reason to believe that Jewish settlements were started in the parts of Eastern Europe which later became Russia. They disappeared except perhaps for a few remnants, which may have lasted until the Middle Ages. The Mongol invasion of the thirteenth century wiped out any trace of them. Except for a lone Jew here and there, there was no Eastern European Jewry until the thirteenth century, when settlement started with people from Bohemia and Germany.

It was Western Europe that became the center of gravity for Jewish life in the Middle Ages. In the centuries that saw the decline of Roman power (350–650), many Jews engaged in farming. As freed slaves, or as poor immigrants seeking a better life, they bought small farms as soon as they could afford it. The incessant warfare and the decline of the cities made the life of a merchant or artisan precarious. So more Jews shifted from commerce to farming. Some became the owners of large estates in Spain, Italy, and southern France.

And then the tide was reversed and Jews were forced to abandon agriculture. The Church, which like everybody else used slave labor on its estates, issued decrees against Jews owning slaves. (Too many slaves were adopting Judaism as a quick path to the freedom Jews were bound by their faith to give fellow Jews in slavery.) Without labor it was impossible to farm the land. Nor could Jews take the religious oath of mutual defense that obligated feudal landlords to protect one another from roving marauders or voracious neighbors. Except for the minority who converted to Christianity to keep their lands, most Jews were forced to give up agriculture.

Luckily, the warfare between the Christians and the Moslems gave the Jews an opening to another way to make a living. The interchange of goods between East and West had been crippled when the Moslems gained control of the eastern coast of the Mediterranean in 650. Because the Jews were not a part of that quarrel, both sides were willing to do business with them. Jewish merchants could come and go freely, using their fellow Jews along the commercial routes to establish trading stations.

"Jew" and "merchant"—in the popular mind the two terms soon came to mean the same thing. But as soon as Christians and Moslems worked out a sort of peace, the Jews no longer monopolized trade. Christians were drawn to where the profits were, and Venetians and other Italians soon rivaled the Jewish merchants. Jews partnered with Christians and together they expanded international trade.

Serving the economic needs of medieval society, the

Jews were protected by the kings and nobles who knew their value and had a stake in their success. As the old towns of Roman days revived and new towns sprang up along the trade routes, the Jews once more came to live chiefly in the urban centers. These were relatively small —perhaps a few thousand Christian families and fifty Jewish families. The Jews could live where they liked, often on streets together with Christians. All Jews lived under the regulations imposed by the Jewish community. Life centered on the synagogue and the cemetery. Leadership came from the elders, who had the authority to judge civil suits between Jews and to levy fines.

It was only in Spain that the Jews of medieval Western Europe experienced a "Golden Age." With the Moslem conquest of Spain came freedom from the slavery they had known under the harsh rule of the Visigoths. Jewish writers of the Middle Ages identified Spain as the Sepharad where Obadiah (verse 20) had prophesied the exiles of Jerusalem would find refuge. The Jews of this Iberian corner of Europe thus came to be known as the *Sephardim*. The contrasting term, Ashkenazim, arose at the same time. Jewish communities had prospered in the Rhineland towns and medieval rabbis began to speak of Germany as Ashkenaz (Genesis 10:3 and Jeremiah 51:27). Gradually the Jews of northern Europe came to be called Ashkenazim to distinguish them from the Sephardim.

Jewish merchants contributed greatly to Spain's rising power and wealth. Prosperous Jews and Moslems alike were proud to foster culture. Hebrew scholarship flowered side by side with the Moslem and the two cooperated in studies and teaching. The cultures inter-mixed through translation of one another's works. Jewish philosophers, poets, physicians, mathematicians, astron-omers, geographers, cartographers, diplomats, trans-lators, and financiers helped fertilize the soil from which the intellectual life of Europe would be reborn.

But beyond the peninsula the Jews of Europe enjoyed no Golden Age. They were only tolerated in the medi-eval centuries. Under the Church's influence, the state made Jews outcasts. King, noble, or bishop controlled their lives. Shut off from the land, they were also ex-cluded automatically by the Christian guilds from the many crafts and trades they had practiced. As the econ-omies developed, the Church eased its restrictions on commercial activity. Trade became more respectable and Christians who had been eyeing the profitable world of trade began to displace the Jews as merchants. The Jews had to turn to banking and finance (the Church still forbade Christians to receive interest) and by 1250 they so dominated the field in many countries that "money-lender" and "Jew" became as synonymous as "mer-chant" and "Jew" had once been. But as this sphere too became enticing, the Church's restrictions relaxed and Christians again replaced Jews. Most medieval Jews knew nothing but poverty; they endured through their tough loyalty to Jewish life and their conviction that it was the only one certain to bring salvation to mankind.

It is worth noting that everywhere, as a country's economy advanced, Jews were permitted only a smaller and smaller role in it. Forced out of Western Europe, they pioneered the commercial development of Eastern

Europe. When they were no longer considered essential to the economy, their Christian rivals called them avaricious and heartless—the image perpetuated by Shakespeare's Shylock—and then took over their functions.

The Crusades, which began in 1095, convulsed the medieval world and were a catastrophe for the Jews. The romantic tales of chivalrous knights fighting to reclaim the Holy City of Jerusalem from the unbelievers omit the horror that accompanied the holiness. For two hundred years the Jews who lived along the path of the eight Crusades felt the murderous effect of armed zeal. What, said the Christian preachers, march to redeem the Holy Land from the infidel and leave untouched these Jewish dogs in our midst? So they sacked and burned the Jewish communities, raped their women, massacred their people. Greed as well as piety inspired the Crusaders. A Jewish merchant or moneylender killed meant goods that could be seized or a debt that could be canceled.

It was in 1215 that the Church's Fourth Lateran Council decreed Jews must wear distinctive dress—a large hat on the head, or a yellow or crimson circle over the heart. They became plainly marked targets for mobs who saw the Jew as the "Christ-killer." Made public pariahs, they seemed certain to be headed for expulsion or extermination. For the first time, stories were spread that Jews murdered Christian children and used their blood for the Passover ritual. (Pagans had accused the early Christians of the same crime of ritual murder.)

But the elimination of the Jews did not happen all at once. As long as their money could be drained into royal treasuries, they were tolerated. Once they lost that value,

In this fourteenth-century French print, Jews wear the circular yellow badge. Louis IX ordered the yellow wheel to be worn both front and back so that Jews could be recognized from every side

they were thrown out: from England in 1290, from France in 1306, from the German countries in the fourteenth and fifteenth centuries, from Spain in 1492.

The shock of expulsion from Spain was the greatest Jews had known since the destruction of the Second Temple. Many Jewish communities of Western Europe disappeared, their people driven to martyrdom, to forced conversion, to emigration. Only a small number of those who fled survived to reach their destination.

What of the Jews who were allowed to remain in Western Europe? After Spain expelled its Jews, the idea spread that Jews must live apart from Christians. Like all people who hold something in common, Jews tended to live near one another. But the choice had been theirs. Now they were compelled to live in a ghetto, behind walls and locked gates. The law forced the Jew to live there and nowhere else, while the Christian could live anywhere but in the ghetto.

Generation after generation—from 1500 to 1800—the Jews were labeled the instrument of Satan and subjected to degrading regulations. They were cut off from the mainstream and isolated. The rights and privileges they had known when they were a vital part of European development were taken away from them. Declared unwanted, they were made unnecessary. "It is impossible," says the Catholic historian Frederick M. Schweitzer, "to narrate medieval Jewish history as anything but a nightmare of horrors—injustice, massacre, expulsion, forcible conversion, contempt, hatred. In a word, it was a perpetual state of terror, one that was not alleviated but deepened with the passage of time."

By 1600 the ghettos had sunk into a squalid darkness. The infinite variety of Jewish life enjoyed in the days of freedom narrowed into rigid custom. Intellectual life could only stagnate in the ghetto. The world outside heaped contempt upon the Jew; it was inevitable that fear and suspicion of everything beyond the walls should color the ghetto Jew's attitude. Although Italy and Germany were the chief enforcers of ghetto existence, the ghetto attitude spread to Jews in other lands.

The birth of Protestantism in the sixteenth century only intensified the evil. Luther fueled the flames of bigotry when he called for the extermination of the Jews. And Catholicism, defending itself against the new Protestant heresies, charged that the Reformation was the product of Jewish influence. It seemed that both wings of Christianity measured religious zeal by how harshly the Jew was treated.

The Jews expelled from Western Europe went in many directions. The English, French, and German refugees headed for Prussia, Austria, Poland, and Lithuania. The Sephardic Jews scattered widely—to the Ottoman Empire (Turkey), to Palestine, to northern Italy, to Holland. And some to the New World, where they settled first in Brazil and the West Indies, and then in North America. Now the Diaspora was worldwide.

But the major migration was from west to east. By 1500 the center of the Jewish world had shifted east of the Rhine. The East European era in Jewish history had begun.

# 2 ORDER AND CHAOS

T HE JEWS MAKING NEW HOMES IN EAST-
ern Europe felt optimistic. First of all, they were
welcomed. Poland and the other Slavic countries were
beginning to stir economically. They were poor compared to Western Europe, but they were moving up.
Their cities were growing. There was a need for Jewish
hands and a need for Jewish enterprise. A Jew could earn
his bread and eat it in peace. Such security after the
hatred and terror suffered in the West drew a deep sigh
from a sixteenth-century rabbi of Cracow. "If it could
only stay this way until the Messiah's arrival!" he wrote.

The Polish Jews were largely artisans and tradesmen.
They practiced many crafts and moved freely in the
channels of commerce. As far back as 1264, one of
Poland's rulers, Boleslav the Pious, had issued a charter
protecting Jews from mistreatment and regulating their
relations with the government and with Christians. The
charter made it possible for Jewish communities to function under Talmudic law. Later, in 1344, Casimir the
Great had expanded the royal safeguards for Jews.

With life, property, and freedom to worship protected, the Jews increased rapidly. By the seventeenth
century there were hundreds of thousands in Poland and
Lithuania. In many towns they were a majority of the

population. Usually they lived in separate quarters, but these were not the walled-in ghettos of the West. They were chosen freely because the people wanted to enjoy the traditional Jewish communal life. Here they could be Jews at home and Jews outside their homes without fear or shame.

Under such favorable conditions the Jews developed a middle class. They were a useful bridge between the owners of the large estates and the peasants who worked the land. They served as agents for the nobles, operating their estates or taking charge of such sources of revenue as inns and taverns. In eastern Poland, particularly on the Ukrainian steppes, Jews herded livestock, planted and fished, and helped make spirits, potash, and flour. They took a major role in trade, distributing farm produce, bringing in textiles and luxuries from abroad, and selling Poland's furs and raw materials. They marketed merchandise throughout the villages and towns, and took part in the fairs vital to the country's commercial growth. As credit became more important to Poland's economic life, the Jews lent money to all classes from king to peasant. (Non-Jews too engaged in the same business.)

Lacking an official system for collecting taxes and tolls and managing state properties, the Polish government put this essential function in the hands of "tax farmers." These private individuals paid the government a fixed sum for a fixed period to carry on the profitable occupation. Jews and non-Jews, burghers and noblemen, took up the business. The Church opposed giving Jews such authority over Christians but couldn't prevent it.

The Jews were not Poland's only immigrants in this

period. German Christians entered too, and in large numbers. Part of their baggage was hatred for the Jews and the conviction that these people had no rights any non-Jew was bound to respect. The German settlers competed with the Jews as merchants and artisans and, where they could, tried to limit Jewish influence. The Church backed such moves to restrict Jews who would not be converted to Christianity. It sought to pressure the government in this direction and to prejudice the peasants and the townfolk against their Jewish neighbors.

But because the kings and nobles felt they could not do without the Jews' economic services, the opposition did not get very far. True, the charge of ritual murder was often revived and there were some bloody outbreaks in the cities. But the villages where many Jews lived were quiet. The terror unleashed against the Jews of the West during the sixteenth century did not sweep over Poland. Now and then Jews were banished from one city or another. Still, under royal Polish protection, Jewish immigrants continued to arrive from Western Europe.

The refugees brought with them the patterns of communal life that had developed widely among medieval Jews. A governing body called the *kahal* headed the Jewish community. It maintained a synagogue and cemetery, a ritual bath, a hospital and home for the aged, and distributed charity funds to sustain the needy. Poland's rulers allowed the kahal to manage Jewish affairs. It collected the taxes for transmittal to the government. Since the richer paid the greater part, they came to exercise the greater power. Committees took care of economic, legal, and educational matters. The Jews had their own judicial system, appointed their own rabbinical judges, and enforced their own decisions. The great fairs which dominated Polish economic life provided the opportunity for the lay and religious leaders of Jewry to meet regularly. These meetings led to the formation of a Parliamentary Council of the Four Lands, which grew into a complex instrument for governing the affairs of all the Jews in the kingdom.

It was their community organization that helped the Jews to develop their economic strength. It protected Jewish commercial interests in two ways. It acted for all Jews in dealing with the world outside—the kings, nobles, and burghers—seeking to win from them privileges or agreements. At the same time, it tried to reduce competition among the Jews themselves and to maintain fair trading practices within Jewry and in dealings with non-Jews.

The expansion of commerce spurred the growth of handicrafts. In the early 1600's Jewish merchants saw the possibilities of trade in ready-made clothing. They sold craftsmen raw material on credit. The tailors made up the garments and sold them back to the merchants at a low price. (This was the putting-out system, an early stage in capitalism.) The use of credit enabled many Jews to enter the garment trade. The second most important industry for them was baked goods, but they spread into many other trades too, both light and heavy.

Soon the craftsmen were numerous enough to organize their own guilds, like those of the Christians. Their aim was to better their economic position by controlling competition. Cracow's seven Jewish master barbers (Sender, Shmerl and his brother, Hirsch, Hayyim, Moses, and Jehiel) formed a guild in 1639. Unlike the barbers of today, they also did a good deal of minor surgery. These passages from their guild laws indicate their concerns:

1. First, they are obligated to make a weekly collection for charity among their members, receiving as much as the generous instincts of each one prompts him to give.

2. No barber may keep in his shop more than one apprentice to teach the trade to. This apprentice must bind himself for three successive years. During the first two years the apprentice shall under no circumstances be permitted to bleed a patient; and even in the third year he shall not be allowed to let blood except when his master is at his side. This is in order that he may practice and accustom himself to the work properly, and not faint or become slipshod in his profession . . .

5. The above mentioned barbers have also bound themselves not to raise prices and thus impose a burden upon the people of our community, but will accept the fee that people have been accustomed of old to pay for bloodletting, cupping, hair cutting, and the healing of bruises and wounds, so as not to give rise to any complaint against themselves on the part of the people of our community. On the other hand they will not cheapen or lower—God forbid—their fees by being too liberal, and forgoing that which is

*their just due by accepting less than one Groschen net from everyone for cupping. Whoever will transgress by treating the matter of fees lightly will always have to give to charity, as an unquestioned obligation, a half a gulden, not to mention other punishments, and both he and anyone he may send will be prevented from doing any more work . . .*

*11. The seven barbers above mentioned have also agreed that there shall be brotherliness and friendship among themselves, and that during the three festivals they will have a good time, enjoy themselves to the full, and be glad and merry of heart . . .*

The scholarship of Polish Jews won recognition far beyond the borders of the country. Jews abroad sent their sons to study the Talmud in Polish *yeshivas*. The Talmud was not only a sacred religious work but a practical guide to everyday life. Its scholars held sway in the religious schools and also in the public assemblies and kahal councils. The increasing complexity of economic and social life provided students of the Talmud with new legal problems to test their creativity.

By a natural process, the language of the Jews of Poland became Yiddish. Jews everywhere had always spoken the language of their homeland—Arabic, French, Italian, Spanish, whatever it was. They also knew the languages of the Bible and their sacred writings—Hebrew and Aramaic. In medieval Germany the Jews had spoken a Middle High German, with a Hebrew admixture. They continued to use it when they migrated eastward, now mixing in Slavic words too. By the sixteenth century this Yiddish tongue had become the common speech of Jews throughout Eastern Europe. A popular literature in Yiddish flourished, with Cracow as its publishing center.

Compared with the agony they had known in the Western countries, life in Poland was calm for the Jews. They were now the largest Jewish community in Europe. The Roman Catholic clergy continued to harass them, but still they prospered. Then overnight, in the year 1648, everything changed. Civil war broke out in Poland. Greek Orthodox Cossacks from north of the Black Sea rose up in revolt. They were led by Bogdan Chmielnitsky, who united the Ukrainian peasants and the Tatars against the "heretical" Roman Catholic Poles and the "unbelieving" Jews. It was a war of extermination. The Cossacks had been badly treated by their Roman Catholic Polish lords. The Ukrainian peasants. blamed the Jewish tax farmers for the heavy burden placed on them to satisfy the greedy demands of the Polish nobles. Economic grievances and religious hatred combined to bring the Jews catastrophe.

On June 10, 1648, the Cossacks moved on the town of Nemirov in Podolia. Here many Jews from the countryside had gathered for protection under the fortress walls. Nathan Hannover, a Polish rabbi, describes what he saw happen:

> When the Jews saw the troops from afar they were frightened, though as yet they did not know whether they were Polish or Cossack. Nevertheless the Jews went with their wives and infants, with their silver and

*gold, into the fortress and locked and barred its doors,
ready to fight them. What did those scoundrels, the
Cossacks, do? They made flags like the Poles, for there
is no other way to distinguish between the Polish and
the Cossack forces except through their banners. Now
the people of the town, although they knew of this
trick, nevertheless called to the Jews in the fortress:
"Open the gates. This is a Polish army which has
come to save you from your enemies, should they
appear."*

*The Jews who were standing on the walls, seeing
that the banners were like the flags of the Polish forces
and believing that the townspeople were telling them
the truth, immediately opened the gates to them. No
sooner had the gates been opened than the Cossacks
entered with drawn swords, and the townsmen too,
with swords, lances, and scythes, and some only with
clubs, and they killed the Jews in huge numbers. They
raped women and young girls; but some of the women
and maidens jumped into the moat near the fortress
in order that the Gentiles should not defile them and
were drowned in the water. Many of the men who were
able to swim also jumped into the water and swam,
thinking they could save themselves from slaughter.
The Russians swam after them in the water. Some of
the enemy, too, kept on shooting with their guns into
the moat, killing them till finally the water was red
with the blood of the slain.*

Rabbi Hannover's father died in the slaughter that
year and he himself was murdered later. Six thousand

Jews were killed in Nemirov. Those who escaped fled to Tulchin, only to be handed over to the Cossacks by Polish nobles who thought to buy their own safety with Jewish blood. After killing the Jews, the Cossacks killed the Poles.

The wars went on for ten years—Cossacks, Tatars, and then Muscovites and Swedes invading Poland and Lithuania one after another. The Muscovites too massacred Jews, or drove them to the Russian interior, where they were made to convert or sold into slavery. Poland was forced to give up most of the Ukraine to Russia. Hundreds of Jewish communities were wiped out. Hundreds of thousands—over one third of the total Jewish population—died by sword, famine, and pestilence. All Polish Jewry was impoverished. A tide of refugees swept westward, a tide that would persist under persecutions extending into the twentieth century. Jewish suffering in wave after wave of pogroms reached a peak unparalleled until the time of Hitler. "Now, at least," wrote one Jewish scholar, "every single Jew knew without any doubt that the Messiah was coming, for he had to come."

The "deluge" is the name given this period in the history of Poland. The uprisings and wars were ruinous. Anarchy and corruption ruled the country. And the worse things were for Poland, the worse they were for the Jews. Competition between Jew and non-Jew became the more intense, and persecution and pogrom the more frequent. The enormity of the national disaster made Jews feel hopeless about their prospects here on earth. As in the past, whenever the hardships of their lives as Jews deepened, they turned to mysticism and asceticism.

The study of *Cabala*—Jewish mysticism—became popular again. Jews took the troubles of the time as proof that the messianic era was near, for it had been foretold that the Messiah's coming would be preceded by war and pestilence. In 1648 Sabbatai Zevi, a magnetic young Jew of Smyrna, announced himself as the Messiah and declared the millennium would begin in 1666. The Jews of Europe, desperate for a miraculous deliverance from persecution, welcomed the news with frenzied joy. In that year, as he had promised his adherents, Sabbatai Zevi came to Constantinople to force the Sultan of Turkey, ruler of the Holy Land, from his throne and to lead the dispersed remnants of Israel back to Mount Zion to establish the Kingdom of God. But the sultan clapped him into a dungeon and offered him the choice of converting to Islam or losing his head.

Sabbatai Zevi turned Mohammedan. His apostasy was a betrayal, a shattering disillusionment for his followers. They sank into deeper despair. They had learned how to live as Jews in the Diaspora—the Talmudic texts taught them that—but was it enough? How long must they wait for deliverance? The messianic fervor indicated many could no longer resign themselves to accept this life. In the anarchy which had seized Poland, the moral strength of the community leaders and the rabbis was crippled. They were helpless in the face of such widespread disaster.

Just now, when their spirit was failing, a religious movement began which had a great and profound effect upon the Jews. Its founder was Israel ben Eliezer, known among his followers as the Besht (from the first letters of the three Hebrew words *Baal Shem Tov*, Master of the Good Name). He was born about 1700 in the province of Podolia, at the foot of the Carpathian Mountains. He started to preach his philosophy of faith among the common people, using their language and voicing their needs. He moved among the village Jews, proclaiming his mission of love and joy. "My teaching," he said, "is based on three kinds of love: love of God, love of the *Torah*, and love of man."

An ecstatic mystic, he saw the world as a wondrous emanation of God. God was everywhere, and his presence made the world full of beauty and melody and joy. Man was God's handiwork, and man should live not in tears and despair but with joy and hope and faith. No matter what his afflictions, man was meant by God to laugh, sing, and dance. This was the purest and highest form of prayer. One worshipped God not by prayer or ritual but by simple acts of loving kindness to one's fellow men. In loving man, the faithful demonstrate their love for God.

Love of God to the Baal Shem was higher than all forms of religious worship, even the study of the Torah. To the Talmudists it was shocking to hear the Baal Shem teach that doing good in life was more meritorious in God's eyes than living up to the strict letter of the 613 precepts of the Torah. But too much rationalism, said the Baal Shem, was a threat to true religion.

His optimistic movement, called *Hasidism* (the word means pietism), penetrated deep into the hearts of Jews

Israel Baal Shem Tov, founder of Hasidism

throughout Eastern Europe. Its warmth and humanity were a dynamic countercurrent to the dry, formalistic Judaism that had prevailed since the 1500's.

Out of Hasidism came a new kind of leader, the *zaddik* (saintly man). He appeared at a time when the mass of Jews longed for a messianic figure, someone who could intervene with God on behalf of His children. Long ago Talmudic law had taken away the crown of priesthood and in its place put the crown of learning. The rabbi, after this change, functioned as the learned man who answered his people's questions.

But the zaddik or *rebbe* was more than a guide to his followers. He was like a priest who transmitted the people's petitions to God. The zaddik was the focal point of the Hasidic community. His province became the human concerns of the *shtetl*—work, business, conscription, poverty, sickness, worry, fear. He heard complaints, gave consolation, inspired hope, prescribed joyful love of God. Dynasties of zaddikim developed as leadership came to rest on hereditary authority. A visit to the zaddik at his court was considered to be of great importance. Followers were always close by, but they came especially on the holidays to observe his conduct, listen to his words, and sing and dance with their fellow Hasids.

Martin Buber saw their role this way:

*Through the zaddik all the senses of the Hasid are perfected, not through conscious directing, but through bodily nearness. The fact that the Hasid looks at the zaddik perfects his sense of sight; his listening to him,*

Elijah ben Solomon, the Gaon of Vilna

*his sense of hearing. Not the teachings of the zaddik*
*but his existence constitutes his effectiveness.*

In that same generation another leader arose who saw
the problems of the Jews from a different point of view.
Elijah ben Rabbi Solomon, born in Vilna in 1720, was as
devoted to his people and their faith as the Baal Shem.
A child prodigy, he took the path of restoring vitality to
the study of the law. The faith, hope, and joy of worship
which Hasidism offered he took for granted. Rather than
modify the traditional Judaic attitude toward study, he
called for the fullest development of the Jewish mind as
the way to find an answer to his people's needs. He refused rabbinic posts and gave all his time to study. Soon
he was recognized as the unofficial spiritual leader of
Eastern Europe's Jews, and became known as "the
*Gaon*," a term old Babylonia had applied to the heads of
the academies. The Gaon wanted prayer to be simplified. He was against useless show of mental agility. He
urged concentration on the true meaning and usefulness
of rabbinic wisdom. And as a rationalist he wanted to
restore the harmony that for centuries had existed between Judaism and secular learning. He studied astronomy, physics, mathematics, philosophy, and music. He
thought the mastery of secular knowledge could help
enrich life and broaden the Jew's understanding, not
only of Judaism, but of the world he lived in. "Every
lack of knowledge in secular subjects," he said, "causes a
hundredfold lack in the study of the Torah, for Torah
and knowledge are joined together."

The Jews of Eastern Europe were torn between these

two movements; between the Hasidim and their opponents, called the *Misnagdim*. The masses of southern Poland and the Ukraine formed the base of the Hasidic movement. Northern Poland, with its intellectual tradition, became the stronghold of the Gaon. When the Hasidim began to make inroads in the north, the rabbis met and excommunicated the entire sect, forcing it underground.

The bitterness of the conflict seemed to threaten all Jewry. Just then, the world outside intervened. The kingdom of Poland vanished, dismembered in three stages that lasted over a quarter of a century. After many generations of self-government within their own communities, the Polish Jews found themselves to be the new "Jewish problem" in three strange countries.

# 3 DOUBLY THE ENEMY, DOUBLY THE VICTIM

THE PARTITIONING OF THE COUNTRY speeded the process of change among Poland's million Jews. It did not happen overnight, of course, and it was another quarter century before the boundaries of the states they fell under became fixed.

The first partition began when the Russian troops of Catherine the Great moved into Poland during the Ukrainian uprisings of 1768. The Prussian ruler, Frederick II, fearing the invaders would grab all Poland, proposed the country be divided among the Austrians, the Russians, and himself. When the knife fell in 1772, Russia got the biggest slice—Polish Livonia and White Russia—and about 1.3 million of the inhabitants. Austria got a third of the partitioned land and about half the population. Prussia contented itself with the smallest piece, West Prussia.

A year later Russia forced another partition, this time dividing with Prussia about half of what remained of Poland. In 1795, after the failure of an insurrection for Polish freedom led by Kosciusko, Poland disappeared altogether, carved up once more. Now Russia had her first common frontiers with her fellow partitioners, Austria and Prussia.

After Napoleon won his victory over Prussia in 1806, he altered the map of Eastern Europe again. He carved the semi-independent Duchy of Warsaw out of the portion that had belonged to Prussia since 1793. At the Congress of Vienna the map was redrawn once again. Most of the Duchy of Warsaw, the central part of Poland, became the so-called Kingdom of Poland, attached to Russia. In 1831, when another Polish uprising failed, it was converted into a province. Controlling three fourths of the old Poland, Russia harbored the greater part of Eastern Europe's Jews. All the provinces she had taken during the three partitions (among them the regions of Minsk, Volhynia, Podolia, and Lithuania, with Courland and Bialystok acquired later) were incorporated into Russia proper. From these parts the Jews spread into southern Russia, the Black Sea coast, Bessarabia, and the interior.

Russia's history had begun in the ninth century when Vikings rowed down the rivers from the Baltic to the Black Sea and founded the Principality of Kiev. Within a century, Christianity became the official state religion. It was a slave-trading society. In the twelfth century, colonizers who had cleared the wilderness and wiped out the natives established the Principality of Moscow. From the thirteenth to the fifteenth century, the invading Mongols ruled Russia. After they were driven out, the first independent Russian state was set up, with Moscow as the capital city, and the title of Czar or Caesar came into use for the Russian monarch. Peter the Great (1682–1725) dragged Russia into the Western world, transforming the country's culture, expanding her frontiers, and building the new capital, St. Petersburg, as his window to the West. Catherine the Great, in adding much of Poland to the empire, brought almost a million Jews into a country that had traditionally feared and hated outsiders ever since the Mongol invasion. It was not Jews alone who were distrusted—they were so few until her time—but Mohammedans, Roman Catholics, non-believers.

The Jews entered Russian life as the modern age began for the Jewish world of Europe. Although a few had slipped through the gates earlier, until the arrival of eighteenth-century rationalism, the bulk of the Jews remained prisoners of the ghetto. The ideas of the secular enlightenment, the promise of liberty, equality, and fraternity, were a brilliant attraction to Jewish youth. Outside the dark ghetto the world sparkled with philosophers and scientists, artists and musicians, universities and museums. What was a young Jew starved for culture to choose? Ghetto Judaism or Christian enlightenment? But there was a third choice, a choice dramatized by Moses Mendelssohn.

Born in 1729 to a poor Torah scribe in the ghetto of Dessau, Germany, Mendelssohn made his way to Berlin at fourteen and studied philosophy, mathematics, and languages. While he prospered as a businessman, he earned a great reputation for his critical essays in philosophy. The lion of the intellectual salons, he became Europe's most celebrated Jew. His acceptance in Gentile society led young Jews to dedicate themselves to modern education in the hope they too would achieve a great place in Western culture.

In the same years that the Baal Shem Tov and the Gaon of Vilna were speaking to the needs of Eastern Europe's Jews, Moses Mendelssohn and his followers were seeking to liberate their people from the shackles of the ghetto and to revive the Jewish spirit. The movement was called the *Haskala*, or Enlightenment. Jews must be prepared to meet the challenge of the modern world. Mendelssohn translated the *Pentateuch* into German to make it easier for his fellow Jews to study the Bible. The Haskala wanted the Torah to be taught alongside philosophy and science, and all of them to be used in the search for universal truths. It argued for separation of church and state. It believed religion was the individual's concern. The Jewish community ruled by Talmudic law was like a state within the state, Mendelssohn said, and he warned that modern nationalism would not tolerate that.

Soon after Mendelssohn's death (1786), the French Revolution exploded. Napoleon's armies breached the walls of Europe's ghettos. But inside those ghettos, Jewish communal life, with its own rabbinical laws, courts, and administration, was going on as before. Napoleon believed this to be a feudal remnant that had no place in the new political state. He forced the Jews to convoke an assembly—the first *Sanhedrin* since the destruction of Jerusalem. He instructed the rabbis to renounce the ghetto's Talmudic laws and pledge allegiance to the state and its laws. This the assembly did, leaning on the Talmudic injunction that the laws of the host state were the laws of the Jews, so long as no law violated freedom of religion. Thus Napoleon broke ghetto power and overnight made the Jews citizens, with all the rights and duties of the dominant majority.

It meant a great change for the Jews in the Diaspora. Now they were no longer a minority nation within each country but individual citizens of the state. The new democratic regimes said, in effect, there is no need for Jewish self-government when we guarantee the protection of our minorities. The Talmud, which had been the judicial bulwark of the Jewish communal governments in the Diaspora from Roman through feudal times, seemed endangered. And so too, as events proved, was Jewish identity, for emancipation demanded the renunciation of any Jewish identification but the religious. More and more young Jews deserted the ghetto to warm themselves in the bright sun of Western culture.

But it was different in Eastern Europe. Here, in Russian Poland and the neighboring lands, Jews lived under a benighted government and among backward peoples. Most of Russia's population was rural in 1800. Scarcely 4 percent of the people lived in towns. The upper class, the gentry, were only 1 percent. They included almost everyone with a secular education as well as plenty of ignoramuses. The clergy were another 1 percent. Then, in overlapping categories, there were the military, the merchants, the officials.

The status of the gentry and the peasantry was hereditary by law. The gentry and the clergy were privileged classes, for they were exempt from conscription, taxation, and corporal punishment. The landed gentry had the additional pleasure of levying all three of these upon the peasants on their own estates.

The czars cared nothing for ideals or the rights of man. Their feudal society might have been smashed and the country modernized if Napoleon's campaign against Russia had succeeded. But it failed and the old classes stayed in power. Only a few of them had been educated in Western Europe; the rest were far behind. The Jews had little to learn from the non-Jews. They could draw only upon their own cultural resources and their ancient tradition of learning. They did not feel lonely or isolated, for their number was far larger than in Mendelssohn's Germany. Since there was little to envy or emulate in the Russian world, they did not burn to be accepted as equals by the Christians.

The three states that had swallowed up Poland—Russia, Prussia, and Austria—contained among them nine tenths of Europe's Jews. Their monarchs formed the Holy Alliance at the Congress of Vienna in 1815. With Napoleon's defeat, the Alliance set out to restore whatever the French Revolution had overthrown. They meant to stamp out radical ideas and put the throne and the Church in the place of freedom. Their ideal was a strong national state that would force the minority peoples under its rule to assimilate. As Christian monarchs, they would not tolerate non-Christians. Jews they considered both alien and anti-Christ, hence doubly their enemy, doubly their victim.

Russian policy toward the Jews was changeable and contradictory. Sometimes the government headed in two directions at once; at other times it suddenly reversed itself. Whatever the policy of the moment, it rested solely on force. Usually it met passive resistance from the Jews. The Russian officials charged with carrying out policy might ignore or reinterpret it, either because they were bribed or because they had their own notion of the right policy.

While the government berated the Jews for their separatism, it did its best to keep Jews out of Russian society unless they converted. In effect, the Russian way of "solving the Jewish problem" was to treat this people like the plague, a plague that must be quarantined. In the vast interior of Russia, there were few middle-class people to develop the country's vast resources. It would have been to the government's advantage to encourage the Jews to settle throughout Russia and put their energies to work serving its economic needs. But the merchants of Moscow wanted no competition from Jews. So orders went out barring Jews from living in the interior cities. Czar Alexander I decided to confine the Jews within an even smaller area. He mapped a Pale of Settlement that permitted Jews to live only in a prescribed region—parts of Lithuania, the old Polish provinces, White Russia, and the Ukraine. It was the ghetto again, but on an outsize scale. The rigid policy of segregation was designed to save the "Holy" Russian people from contamination by the Jews.

In all three states of the Holy Alliance the policies on the Jews were similar. Prussia and Austria, like Russia,

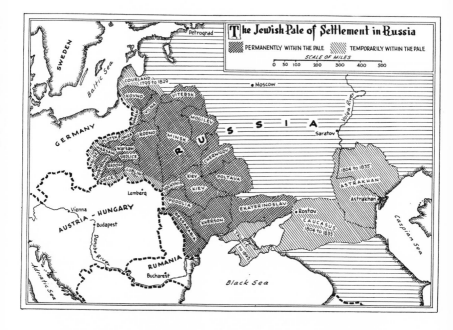

The Jewish Pale of Settlement in Russia

PERMANENTLY WITHIN THE PALE  TEMPORARILY WITHIN THE PALE

SCALE OF MILES

0  50  100  200  300  400  500

set up pales of settlement to keep the Jews out of their interior. They treated the small number of rich or assimilated Jews one way (they were "useful") and the vast mass of the poor Jews quite another (they were "useless"). They forced Jews out of the villages and cut down their trade with the people. Sometimes they tried to switch Jews into different occupations, especially agriculture, but usually they made a mess of it. Jews have to be made more "useful," they would cry, by which they meant, made to pay more and higher taxes. As their states tended toward a degree of modernization, influenced by the spreading demand for democracy and freedom, the notion of graded emancipation was introduced.

The rich Jews were allowed a taste of equality and the poor Jews none. By and large, Russia lagged behind the others when it came to any liberal practices.

The Pale of Settlement was only one part of the Jewish Statute of 1804. The statute was Russia's first comprehensive legislative program for the Jews. It was the product of many sources—high officials, the gentry, proposals sent in by Jews and non-Jews, a special committee, and the example of Prussian laws. It ended up a contradictory mishmash. It called for the expulsion of the Jews from the villages; allowed Jewish children to attend the general schools and Jews to open their own secular schools (with either Russian, Polish, or German as the required language); permitted Jews to buy or rent land for farming; gave Jewish merchants, artisans, and manufacturers permission to live temporarily in the interior, including Moscow and St. Petersburg. It also affirmed the Jews' traditional right to local self-government, with the *kehilla*'s jurisdiction limited to religious affairs.

One provision of the czar's statute obliged Jews to acquire surnames. Up to then the Jews of Eastern Europe had generally been known by their Hebrew names. (In ancient and medieval times, however, Jews had assumed the Greek, Roman, Arabic, Spanish, Gallic, or German names of the regions they lived in.) When there was more than one Jew in the locality with the same name, the name of the father was added. Thus, Aaron the son of Benjamin could be distinguished from Aaron the son of Gideon. When there were two Aarons and each had a father named Benjamin, the occupation of each was often used to make the distinction. Thus, Aaron the blacksmith was differentiated from Aaron the cobbler. Many Jews in Eastern Europe had nicknames tied to personal peculiarities, perhaps to help establish identity. Sometimes the street or town where a man lived, or the name of his wife or mother, was inserted to pin down his identity. Thus "Zalman, Leah's," meaning Zalman, the husband of Leah, might be the way this Zalman was known in a town where a number of men were named Zalman.

The Russian officials did not dictate how family names were to be chosen. "Each family selected the name it liked best," said Dr. Benjamin Lee Gordon in his autobiography. "When Dr. Solomon Mandelkern visited me . . . he told me that he well remembered the time when the ukase came forcing the adoption of a surname. It arrived on a holiday, and there were *mandlen* (almonds) on the table; hence his father's choice. The names Diamond, Gold, Silver, Stein, etc., were adopted by the Jews themselves. In Austria, however, the Jews had no right to select unapproved names. A list of such names was submitted to them, including some very offensive ones, such as Eselkopf, Rundskopf, Ochesenschwanz, Lumpe, Fresser, Schnapser, Grokerklotz, and Wantz."

In the next few years the government banned Jews from holding any leases on land, from selling liquor or keeping taverns, saloons, or inns. (The nobility had blamed the miserable state of the peasantry on the Jewish tavernkeepers.) At one blow a great number of Jews were deprived of their traditional means of livelihood. Expelling Jews from the villages was postponed a few times and, when finally ordered, proved impossible to carry out. So it was put off once again.

In 1818 the government said it was ready for a Jewish advisory body, to be elected by the Jewish communities. The advisers may have had advice to offer, but no one listened. Meanwhile, Jews were ordered not to hire non-Jewish domestics, and their dealings with the village landowners were further limited. Again the order to expel the Jews from the villages came down, was postponed, came down again, was postponed again. In 1823 the now classic drama of a ritual murder trial was staged, this time in the town of Velizh, and two years later the impotent Jewish advisory body was dissolved.

This marked the end of the reign of Alexander I. As the historian Ronald Hingley summed him up, he was a man who "mouthed high-minded abstractions about equality and brotherly love, while contriving to sponsor the continued enslavement and repression" of his subjects. His reign was a busy time for legislative and administrative measures dealing with the Jew. What the Jew learned from it was that he could count on nothing. The government's actions were inconsistent and unpredictable. How could he know where it was safe to live? Or by what trade or profession he could earn his bread? The czar said yes today and no tomorrow. And the next czar?

# 4 CONSCRIPTS FOR
# THE CZAR'S ARMY

THE NEXT CZAR WAS NICHOLAS I. MADE a colonel in his cradle and a general at the age of twelve, he was interested in little but military matters. A notorious martinet, he never wore civilian dress. He inherited a corrupt and disorganized state desperately in need of reform. Educated Russians, most of them army officers, had organized a conspiratorial movement. It did not want simply a palace coup, replacing one despot with another. Rather it had the revolutionary goal of changing the system of government, putting a republic in its place, or at least a constitutional monarchy. The plotters struck in December 1825, when Alexander I died. Badly led, they were dispersed by artillery. Nicholas arrested three thousand Decembrists, as they were called, hung five of their leaders, and exiled hundreds to Siberia.

The answer Nicholas gave to the cry for reform was not more freedom but more discipline. That, and a new national anthem:

> *God save the Czar!*
> *Mighty and powerful,*
> *May he reign in glory over us,*

*Reign that our foes may quake.*
*O Orthodox Czar!*
*God save the Czar!*

He clapped civil servants, professors, and students into distinctive uniforms, elaborated a system of censorship, and created a secret political police called the Third Section. A systematic campaign of thought control began. Nicholas trusted no one but himself. His rigid discipline crushed initiative and silenced criticism. Under the thirty-year rule of this "Iron Czar" (1825–55) the governmental system could only continue to rot and crumble.

While still a Grand Duke, Nicholas had made a tour of Russia. He returned convinced that the Jews he had seen were nothing but "leeches." As czar, his first move against this "internal enemy" was typical—a military measure. Nicholas ordered military conscription for them in 1827, and at a rate double that of the Christian population. And why not double? Weren't they taxed doubly in other respects?

For Jews to be allowed into army service in other countries was considered a privilege (by the Jews, as well). But the term of service in the Russian Army was then twenty-five years. And Nicholas's motives for conscripting Jews were hardly democratic. He wanted to reduce the number of Jews by forcing them to change their religion. If the Jewish soldiers were Russified in their long service, he hoped those who survived would Russify other Jews when they returned home.

Military service normally began at the age of eighteen.

Nicholas thought that was late to begin ridding the Jewish soldier of his "superstitions." He lowered the age for Jewish conscripts to twelve, thus imposing on the children an extra six years of preparation for army life.

During the years from twelve to eighteen, the children were farmed out to Russians in the remote interior, where ordinarily Jews were not allowed to set foot. There they worked the soil and were trained in the proper faith. Then at eighteen they began their twenty-five-year service.

Upon the Jewish kahal was imposed the burden of supplying the young conscripts. (No one volunteered, of course.) Each kahal appointed deputies to do the recruiting. As the season for recruitment approached, many of the children and young men marked for service disappeared. A Yiddish folk song recalls it:

*Az aleksander pavlovitsh iz meylech gevorn,*
*Zenen yidishe hertser freylech gevorn, oyvey, oyvey!*
*Der ershter ukaz iz aropgekumen oyf yidishe zelner,*
*Zenen zich ale tselofn in di puste yelder, oyvey, oyvey!*

> *When Nicholas I became king,*
> *Jewish hearts became "gay," oh, woe!*
> *The first decree for Jewish soldiers was issued,*
> *Then all fled to the wild woods, oh, woe!*

Into the forest or across the border they fled, hunted like animals. In hiding they lived a nightmare, waiting for the whisper of an informer. Since the physically unfit were rejected, another route of escape was self-mutilation. Men amputated fingers and toes, deafened their ears, blinded their eyes, rather than enter the hated service. Mary Antin, who came from Polotzk, wrote of still another way out:

> It was always possible to bribe conscription officers. This was a dangerous practice—it was not the officers who suffered most in case the negotiations leaked out—but no respectable family would let a son be taken as a recruit till it had made every effort to save him. My grandfather nearly ruined himself to buy his sons out of service . . .
>
> If it were cowardice that made the Jews shrink from military service they would not inflict on themselves physical tortures greater than any that threatened them in the army, and which often left them maimed for life. If it were avarice—the fear of losing the gains from their business . . . they would not empty their pockets and sell their houses and sink into debt on the chance of successfully bribing the Czar's agents . . .

Resistance to the draft meant the Jewish community had trouble meeting its quotas. The czar was ruthless: for every missing Jew he ordered three others to be taken. Anyone who hid a runaway or helped him escape was himself punished by military service, and his community made to pay a heavy fine. If the deputies failed to fill their quota, they could be fined or inducted.

The czar's elaborate conscription law with its ninety-five clauses gave many openings for corruption. Parents could save their own sons by supplying a substitute who had to be a Jew. It meant a ready market for kidnappers. Another clause let a town turn in as a recruit any Jew caught away from home without a passport. Jewish gangsters roved the highways and invaded the inns, attacked lone Jews, tore up their papers, and delivered them for a price to the nearest recruiting station.

Many parents tried to keep the birth of their sons a secret. They did not register the newborn. Such unregistered boys were known as *malochim*—angels. They lived, but yet, because of the government's cruelty, they did not exist.

Luckless parents had to stand by and see their children herded off to the eastern provinces and Siberia. It was like mourning for the dead: they would be gone at least a quarter of a century, if not forever. The Hebrew writer I. L. Levin, who saw such a transport start on its long journey, described the scene:

> *Near a house stood a large and high wagon, to which a pair of horses were harnessed. Soldiers brought out children from the house, one after another, and deposited them in the wagon. Soon it was packed to capacity. Children were sitting or lying on top of each other like herring in a barrel. Fathers, mothers, and relatives stood around. A person who has not seen the agonizing parting of parents from their little children and who has not heard their helpless lamentations that penetrate to heaven does not know real tragedy. One father gives his boy a little book of Psalms. Another hands his son phylacteries. From all*

*sides are heard admonitions: "Remain a Jew; no mat-*
*ter what happens, hold fast to Jewishness!" Mothers*
*wring their hands, the hopeless tears never stop,*
*moans of agony and cries of despair resound. I was*
*then nine. I kept looking at the sky. I felt that now, at*
*any moment, God must perform a miracle. He must*
*rain down pitch and tar upon the murderers. He must*
*scatter them, so that the imprisoned children could*
*return to their mothers . . . But the sky remained*
*calm, and the wagon began to move to the accom-*
*paniment of piercing cries and shouts.*

The officers in charge were instructed to carry the
children by wagon. But sometimes they pocketed the
transport money and soon after leaving the village would
drive the children on foot the rest of the way. The
records show such journeys on foot to the remote regions
could take a full year, the children slogging month after
month through dust, mud, snow, ice, beaten with the
knout, starving, sickening, dying. The Russian revolutionary Alexander Herzen, while serving a sentence in
exile, once came across such a group of Jewish children.
He spoke to their transport officer:

> *"Whom are you escorting and to where?"*
> *"As you see—a horde of damned little Jews, eight to*
> *ten years of age. At first, they were supposed to be*
> *driven to Perm; then the order was changed. We're*
> *driving them to Kazan. I took charge of them for a*
> *hundred versts. The officer who handed them to me*
> *said, 'It's a misfortune—a third of them remained on*

*the road (the officer pointed his finger downward).*
*Not half will reach their destination. They die like*
*flies!"*

*The children were lined up in proper formation. It*
*was one of the most terrible sights I have ever wit-*
*nessed. Poor, unfortunate children! The 12-and 13-*
*year-old lads were still holding up, somehow. But the*
*little ones, of eight and ten! . . . No brush could*
*create such horror on canvas . . . Pale, exhausted,*
*frightened, they stood in their clumsy army overcoats,*
*eyeing pitifully and helplessly the soldiers who lined*
*them up roughly. Their lips, their eyes, indicated how*
*feverish they were. Gusts from the Arctic Sea blew in.*
*Without care or help they were marching on—on*
*toward their graves . . .*

Even children as young as eight were taken. If they
weren't married, they could be snatched off the street
and sent into the army at any age. Jews had to find a way
out, and boys still at the age to be playing marbles were
married to little girls. Folk humor includes a story about
a Jew who saw such a child playing on the street and
asked him why he wasn't at school. The child answered,
"I don't go to school any more. I was married yesterday."

"If you got married yesterday and are now the head of
a family, why aren't you wearing long pants?"

"Yesterday I got married, so I wore the pants; today
my little brother is getting married, so he's wearing the
pants."

What happened to the Jewish children who reached
the distant barracks? They were formed into battalions

and their religious retraining begun. Every means was tried to induce them to convert. The local priest worked on them, and when he failed, as he usually did, the noncommissioned officers turned to force. A favorite method was to make the child kneel on the barracks floor when bedtime came. If he consented to be baptized, he was allowed to sleep in his bed. If not, he was kept on his knees all night, until he collapsed. The stubborn ones were beaten or tortured. If they refused to eat pork, they suffered more beatings. They were fed on salted fish and then denied water unless they agreed to baptism. Most of the younger ones gave up and were baptized. The older children often endured the whippings, the hunger, the thirst, the sleeplessness, refusing to betray their faith. Some who would not yield were whipped to death, some were drowned.

"The Gentiles used to wonder at us," said Mary Antin, "because we cared so much about religious things—about food, and Sabbath, and teaching the children Hebrew. They were angry with us for our obstinacy, as they called it, and mocked us and ridiculed the most sacred things." When her cousin was taken as a soldier, his company was briefly stationed in Polotzk. "I saw my cousin drill on the square, carrying a gun, *on the Sabbath*. I felt unholy, as if I had sinned the sin in my own person. It was easy to understand why mothers of conscript sons fasted and wept and prayed and worried themselves to their graves."

Zalman Shazar, a writer who later became president of Israel, tells of the poet Yaakov Shalom Katzenelenbogen, called Yashak, who came from Shazar's home town of Steibtz. Two weeks after he was conscripted, Yashak fled from the army and, still in his uniform, came straight to the Shazar home:

*He had not given a thought to what might happen to him, but as soon as we learned that he had gone off without leave and that everyone, including the police, had seen him rushing through the streets of the town, we understood the grave danger to which he was exposing himself. The family had not even been able to discuss where best to hide him, when the police appeared; and the police, two Christian constables and their Jewish assistants, had not even crossed our threshold, when Yashak jumped through a window and ran out. He fled, and the police raced after him. Panic-stricken, the townspeople watched the young man they were so fond and proud of—this prodigy of traditional and modern learning . . . running for dear life down the streets, pursued by two corpulent armed policemen, who blew their whistles and shrieked: "Catch him! Catch him!" while after them, running and stumbling and ostensibly shouting, trailed the Jewish policeman with the shiny tin badge on his chest. The vague phrase, "running away from the army," had suddenly become terribly concrete for all us onlookers; it was like a deer fleeing from hunters in a forest.*

*Naturally no one of all the townspeople so much as lifted a finger to catch the fugitive; but they did* nothing to help him either: fear of the authorities was simply too strong. They stood there petrified, staring at the ghastly spectacle. Only the Jewish policeman turned aside for a second and slipped into our house, whispering something to my sister and hastily returning to the chase. A few minutes later my sister handed me her little valise packed with some of her clothing and told me to carry it to the shed in her friend's yard. All this while Katzenelenbogen was still running like an arrow speeding through the air along the synagogue street straight to the market, with the policemen at his heels. In the market place he jumped onto the railing of my uncle's house and from the railing into the courtyard and from the courtyard into the garden, the policemen whistling and shouting after him all the time. And then in the garden he climbed on the fence, jumped up into a tree and then into another tree—and vanished.

Half an hour later Reuvele the waggoner drove his carriage in leisurely fashion through the town. His passengers were three girls: one was my sister; the second, her friend, the daughter of our wealthy man and granddaughter of Yashak's mother's new husband; and between them sat an elegant young lady, dressed like the daughter of a Polish nobleman—with a hat and parasol. Along the synagogue street, then across the Nieman River, the carriage travelled, heading toward the tar furnaces that belonged to our wealthy man.

From those tar furnaces young Katzenelenbogen

*made his way to the border, and from the border to Lvov, and from Lvov to London. We were never to see him again . . .*

An organization to rescue children forced into military service was created by Rabbi Menaham Mendel Schneersohn, head of the Habad dynasty of Hasids for nearly forty years. Where his underground railroad could not operate, he instituted a secret program to steel the children's resolve to remain faithful Jews.

The Jewish soldiers who survived knew little but humiliation and cruelty in service. As a rule they were not trained for combat but made to serve as orderlies or musicians. It was a lonely life, separated from family and community. Even if they adapted to this alien world, they could never win promotion to commissioned officer. A high proportion of those who completed their service ended it as invalids, and returned to civilian life still second-class citizens. In Western Europe, army service brought the Jewish soldier equal rights. Not in Russia.

Morris R. Cohen, who became a distinguished philosopher, wrote of his childhood in the town of Neshwies. He recalled the frequent visits to his home of the water carrier . . .

*. . . an old man who had been a soldier under Czar Nicholas. He had been taken away from home as a very young boy, kept in some sort of non-Jewish institution until he was 18 and then served 25 years in the Russian army, his regiment participating in the*

*Crimean War. After his discharge he returned to Neshwies, married, and on his meager earnings as a water-carrier, brought up two adopted children of whom he frequently spoke. Whenever he came to the house to deliver water, he and my grandfather would exchange stories—often the same ones—but I listened with rapt attention to the discussion between the two old men in regard to former days—the incidents of the Crimean War, of the Polish uprisings of 1832 and 1836, of the Turkish War of 1878, and what happened to the Jews during these and other days . . .*

The burden of military service fell upon the poorer Jews. Merchants, shop superintendents, rabbis, graduates of Russian schools were spared duty, although they had to pay a thousand rubles if exempted. In one town the poor Jews smashed the windows of the rich because they saw the deputies were recruiting none of them.

When the czar's conscription plan turned the kahal into police dogs tracking down recruits, it created professional informers. These *moserim* became a plague. They threatened to inform against the kahal whenever it took steps to avoid or lighten the draft by such measures as false registration. They demanded bribes in return for silence.

A gang of these informers operated in Minsk. One of their victims was the father of Ephraim Lisitzky, who tells what happened:

*When it came time for my father to serve in the hated Russian army of the Czar, his widowed mother, whose sole support my father was at the time, hit on the idea of changing his elder brother's name, and entering him in the town's death records. This imaginary death earned my father the right, as the first-born, to be exempted from military conscription.*

*Unluckily for him, however, my father passed from the frying pan of military service into the fire of the informers. Those scoundrels learned of my grandmother's ruse after a few years, and proceeded to make my father's life miserable. Under the threat of denouncing him to the authorities, they extorted money from my father. They visited our home from time to time. Loudly, banging their fists on the table, they would yell: "We're assessing you so much and so much. You deliver it by such and such a date or we turn you in!" Vainly my father and mother pleaded with them to have mercy; they had to hand the money over on the scheduled day—money they had saved by stinting on food or pawning their few possessions.*

*One day the informers dropped in on my mother when she was alone and told her they were holding my father at one of their hideouts, and they would hand him over to the police if she didn't pay up within an hour. My mother was pregnant at the time, in the seventh month. Her heart constricted with anxiety— where was she to get the money? At the moment she went into labor, knelt, and gave birth—to a live child, for once. But she was alone in the house, and fainted during the birth. When she regained consciousness, the infant was dead. My mother recovered physically from this ordeal, but she lost her mind. She pounded the wall all day with her fists, screaming to heaven, throwing dishes at the good women of the neighborhood who came to calm her. She rained blows on the head of my father as well as her own father, who had been summoned from his home in Slutzk. After a short while she came to herself, but the depression never left her until the day she died.*

The blackmailers terrorized communities to the point where assassination became the victims' only means of self-defense. In the neighborhood of Ushitza in 1838 the court indicted eighty of the Jewish elders for murdering two informers. Twenty were sentenced to convict-labor gangs. A few fled before the trial, among them Rabbi Israel Rizhiner, who later founded the rabbinical dynasty in Sadgora, Bukovina.

Evasion of the draft caused such a shortage of Jewish recruits that the furious Nicholas I added new and harsher conscription laws in the early 1850's. He fined the entire Jewish community when they sheltered a fugitive. If a recruit was missing, almost anyone could be taken in his place—the family's father, a relative, or a kahal elder. The czar gave them a terrible choice: either turn kidnapper to replace the missing one, or yourself put on the hated gray uniform and serve as a penal soldier.

In that swamp of force and fraud created by the Russian government, the Jews became demoralized. It was risky to stay in your community and risky to leave. You could be drafted at home and kidnapped on the highway. Any friend might be an informer, any stranger a bandit. Jew was turned against Jew.

The Jewish sense of insecurity in a Gentile world was ancient. Under the terrible new pressures exerted by the czars, it was projected even beyond death. There is a traditional bit of Jewish humor about a young Jew facing conscription into the czar's army. A friend tells him to be cheerful:

> *There's really nothing to be depressed about, if you consider the chances sensibly. You're being taken into the army! Well, one of two things will happen: either there's a war or there isn't. If there isn't, what have you to worry about? But even suppose there is a war, one of two things will happen: either you'll be sent to the front or you won't. If you're not, what is there to worry about? But even suppose you're sent to the front, one of two things will happen: either you'll be wounded or you won't. If you're not, what is there to worry about? But even suppose you're wounded, one of two things will happen: either you'll recover or you won't. If you recover, what is there to worry about? But even suppose you don't recover, one of two things will happen: either you'll be buried in Jewish earth or you won't. If you're buried in Jewish earth, what is there to worry about? But even suppose you're not buried in Jewish earth? Well then, well then . . . well then, brother, you're certainly in one hell of a fix.*

# A BALLAD

Vi er hot genumen dem ershtn
  vort bentshn,
Zenen arayngekumen a fule
  shtub mentshn.

No sooner did he begin to
  pray,
Than a whole crowd of people
  came into the house.

—Yidn, ich veys ir zayt gekumen nit noch veyts un nit
  noch korn,
Ir zayt doch gekumen noch
  mayne yunge yorn!

"Jews, I know you didn't come
  for wheat or corn,
But have come for my young
  life!

Ch'ob nit kayn gelt fun aych
  zich oystsukoyfn,
Di vegn t'ir mir farshtelt, ich
  hob nit vu tsu antloyfn.

I have no money to bribe you
  with,
You have barred all the roads,
  and I have nowhere to run."

M'hot im avekgeleygt af dr'erd,
  di keytn tsu shlisn,
Di letste kapotke hot men im
  f'breklech tsurism.

They put him on the ground
  to bind him in chains,
They tore his only coat to
  shreds.

—excerpted stanzas from a ballad about a young Jew trying to
escape seizure by other Jews (Rubin: *Voices of a People*)

# 5 THE USELESS ONES

S O CONSUMING WAS THE HATRED OF Nicholas I for the Jews, one wonders that he found time for anything else. In his thirty-year reign he issued six hundred decrees against them. Not content with new ideas for persecution, such as his military-conscription plan, he dug up ancient anti-Jewish regulations and applied them mercilessly. The sweeping Jewish statute he announced in 1835 was largely a mass of medieval measures whose rusty edges his bureaucrats polished and sharpened. The Pale of Settlement was shrunk again, thus increasing the number of rural places Jews could not settle in. Synagogues could not be placed near churches. Jews could not use Hebrew or Yiddish in documents or commercial papers. They could not hire Christian domestics unless they segregated them from the Jewish help.

To the recruiting law, which was designed to "save" Jewish souls, Russia added a new means of "redeeming" Jewish spiritual life. The police began a censorship drive against Jewish books. The Jewish books printed in Russia—mostly religious—had been strictly supervised by censors who were apostate Jews. Now the government decided that such books coming in from abroad might be dangerous too. Jews were ordered to bring in to the police all books that had not been screened. Thousands were being forwarded to St. Petersburg when the czar decided it would be easier to burn all "harmful" books on the spot. The books that "trustworthy" rabbis had passed were sent to Vilna or Kiev for the stamp of approval or the touch of the match.

Looking abroad, government officials noted that the Prussians and the Austrians were trying other methods of eliminating the "religious fanaticism and isolation" of their Polish Jews. The czar's council pondered what was wrong at home. The Talmud, they concluded, was the root of the evil. It fostered disdain for the Gentiles and made the Jews look to their kahal for authority, rather than to the official government. Jews were educated by those fanatical *melamdim* who preached intolerance of others. And the traditional clothing worn by the Jews further separated them from the Christian community.

As to measures already tried within Russia, the council gave them poor marks. Conscription was having little effect on Jewish morals or manners. Expulsion from the villages had failed too. Jews were so martyr-minded they could endure the worst persecution. Something different was needed.

The council knew just what medicine to give this stubborn people. First, a cultural dose: set up special schools for its children and eliminate both the *cheders* and the melamdim; ban the wearing of the traditional garb; reform the rabbinate. Then take away Jewish autonomy by abolishing the kahal and reforming the special Jewish tax system. Finally, punish the "useless" Jews (the petty traders and the poor) by taking away the few rights they had and raising their recruitment quota.

Nicholas I was impressed. He told his ministers to launch the program.

To prepare the Jews for school reform, a propagandist was needed to sell them on the czar's good intentions. A German Jew, Max Lilienthal, who ran a Reform school for Jews in Riga, was summoned for the task. But how to convince parents that the government wanted to help their children when those same children were being forced by the thousands into the army? It stood to reason that to baptism in the barracks the czar meant to add baptism in the schools.

When Lilienthal finished his impossible mission to the Pale, he reported that the educational plan would be difficult but not hopeless. A few crown schools for Jews were opened with both Christian and Jewish teachers, supervised by the same mix on local boards. The government's secret intention of ultimately closing the cheders and forcing all the Jewish children into schools under Christian control soon leaked out. The Jews' response was passive resistance.

Meanwhile, the czar began cutting down Jewish communal authority. Self-administration was taken over by the police and the municipal councils—except for the functions of dragging recruits into the army and collecting taxes. These the czar left to the gutted kahal. Reform, Nicholas-style, only added to the harshness of Jewish life.

It is hard to understand how any sane official could have thought otherwise. In dealing with the miserable living standard of the Jews, Nicholas turned to police

A side street in the old section of Warsaw

methods for a solution. It was like putting traffic cops in charge of economy. His police snatched Jews out of the villages, threw them into the cities, ordered them out of the borderland, herded them into the interior.

The senseless back-and-forth movement left some Jews still in the villages, but scarcely a tenth of the total Jewish population. They served the village gentry as grain merchants, tavernkeepers, brokers. But the masses of Jews were funneled into the cities, where they competed desperately with one another for work. Shopkeepers, artisans, and laborers—everyone but a handful of rich merchants—made poor livings, if any. A sensible program to establish masses of Jews as farmers would have helped considerably to improve Jewish economic life. But Nicholas I made only erratic gestures in that direction. About twenty thousand Jews settled on the land, too small a fraction to affect the lives of Russia's 2 million Jews.

In the last years of Nicholas I, Western Europe saw a second emancipation. In 1848 the people of France, Germany, Austria, Italy swept away the reaction that had dominated their countries for some three decades. And Jews joined the revolutionary movements that promised political freedom and civil equality to all.

But the absolutism that was overthrown in the West remained in iron control of Russia. The czar's spies were everywhere, nosing out the faintest whiff of reform. It was plain the autocracy would not tolerate a liberal constitution. It was satisfied with a police state.

In 1850, pushing its assimilation program, the government ordered Jews to stop wearing their traditional clothing. The men were also ordered to cut off their earlocks and the women to stop shaving their heads on the eve of marriage. It was a historical about-face. In the Middle Ages the Jews had been compelled to wear the traditional garb. Now they were compelled not to.

When many Jews refused to obey the edict, the police were unleashed. They inspected Jewish women to see if they had natural hair under their wigs, and they caught men on the streets, snipped off their earlocks, and shredded their long gaberdine coats. Resistance to these imperial orders was especially strong among Hasidic Jews, who fought fiercely to retain Jewish customs.

As the reign of Nicholas I neared its end, another ritual murder trial was staged, this time because of the death of two Russian boys in Saratov. The investigation dragged on for years, resulting in a finding of insufficient evidence against the indicted Jews.

In Austria the 1848 revolution placed Jews on a political seesaw. Their freedoms rose and fell with the fortunes of liberalism. But with the 1867 constitution they won civic equality and political representation. Jews flocked into the state schools and the universities, entering law and medicine in large numbers. With the ending of censorship, the Jewish press flourished. Out of Vienna and Lemberg poured many journals devoted to business, politics, scholarship, and the arts. By 1870 Austria's Jewish population exceeded 600,000.

For Russia, hope of freedom dawned when Nicholas I died in 1855. In St. Petersburg, wrote Peter Kropotkin, "men of the educated classes, as they communicated to one another the news, embraced in the streets." For

Russia's Jews it was good news too. Their Haman had died at last. They had no reason to expect much from his son, Alexander II. The training of the heir to the throne did little to encourage originality or independence of thought. As a young officer of the Guards, however, Alexander had disappointed his father by taking scant interest in military affairs. This, together with a kindly disposition, made his father feel that Alexander lacked the qualities essential for a czar.

When Nicholas I died, Russia was in the midst of the Crimean War, the product of his territorial ambitions in southeastern Europe. Alexander's first year on the throne was given to carrying on the war until the fall of Sevastopol, when he negotiated a peace. His father had sacrificed all human concerns to make Russia an invincible military autocracy. But the Crimean fiasco showed how badly led and badly organized the Russian Army was. It was beaten on its home territory by invading French and British forces that were themselves stupidly generaled.

Enlightened public opinion insisted that social reforms were needed to wipe out the humiliation of defeat and to restore Russia's prestige. The educated classes were eager to help with the work of reform. The new czar, while giving up none of his autocratic power, moved gradually toward reform.

In 1861 he freed about 30 million serfs. He acted against strong opposition from serf owners, who feared losing property without compensation. A long debate took place over the questions of how much land the peasants should get, what land, and how it should be paid for. Conditions differed widely among the 50 million peasant slaves; nearly half belonged to the state, not to private owners. In the end the freed serfs got about the same amount of land they had formerly cultivated for their own maintenance. The landlords were paid by the state, which then exacted payments from the peasants on an installment plan stretching over forty-nine years.

Alexander also modified censorship, liberalized educational policy, and encouraged education for all classes. For a while he even restored autonomy to the universities. Russia was decades behind Western Europe in the great technological changes of the industrial revolution. Alexander encouraged the development of Russia's natural resources and the building of a great railway network to tie his vast regions together. He reorganized the army and navy, set up a new judicial system on the French model, introduced a new penal code and a simplified method of civil and criminal procedure. He granted local self-government with elective assemblies to the rural districts and the larger towns.

When the czar emancipated the serfs, it was reasonable to expect he would free the semi-enslaved 2.5 million Jews. But the Jewish question was not met head-on. It was dealt with in bits and pieces, and again with contradictory policies. Instead of the club, the czar tried the carrot. He continued military conscription of the Jews, but with several modifications. The drafting of children was stopped. But the evil done for decades was not atoned for. The Jewish child-soldiers who had converted were not sent home. They were placed instead in the care of Christians.

Recruitment of Jews would be equalized with that of the general population, the government said. But the heaviest burden was still placed on the "nomadic and unproductive" Jews—that is, the "useless" ones so labeled under the old categories. The changed regulations were less conducive to the practice of kidnapping or of drafting "penalized" Jews.

The Jews took advantage at once of the new educational openings. If they had higher education they could now live outside the Pale, enter certain professions, and hold office. Jewish children went to the state schools in greater and greater numbers. By 1872 they were 15 percent of all students in the Pale. Many went on to the universities, chiefly to study law or medicine. It was thrilling to find themselves free of the old bonds. A Jewish lawyer, V. O. Harkavy, told how he and his friend felt when they were enrolled at Moscow University in 1864:

> *When we came out of the old university building, we crossed to the other side of the street and, respectfully doffing our hats, bowed before the sanctuary that had opened its doors to us and we embraced each other. Proudly we walked home, eager to shout to everyone we met: Have you heard? We are students. All at once it was as though the alienation from the Christians around us had gone. We felt like members of a new society . . .*

Alexander's goal was clear: to merge the Jews with the Russian people, "insofar as the moral condition of the

Jews will permit," as he put it. He was following the same path as his father, but using different tactics. Nicholas had segregated the "useless" Jews, piling penalties upon them for a mode of life he, not they, was responsible for. At the same time he made no concessions to the "useful" Jews. Alexander maintained the same categories, only, instead of punishing the "useless," he dangled promises before those who would be obediently "useful."

The Jews who had already prospered were delighted to be promised some privileges. A group of wealthy St. Petersburg merchants pointed out to the czar that equal rights given to Jews in the West had hastened their assimilation. Logically they should have asked him to grant full equality to all Russia's Jews. Instead, they suggested that if certain rights and privileges were granted to "the best among us"—meaning themselves, of course—it would help carry out the government's goal. Thus, they accepted the czar's separation of their own people into those who deserved to live like humans and those who didn't.

On that principle the government marked three grades of Jews as "useful"—the top class of businessmen, the university graduates, and the artisans. Their wealth, education, and skill could help develop commerce and industry, as well as the military machine. Under Alexander II Russia had extended its domain to the Pacific. It was now a vast colonial empire, covering about a sixth of the earth's land surface. The Jewish businessmen were allowed to move out of the Pale and into the interior cities. Their families and a few artisans and domestics could accompany them. (The privilege of leaving the ghetto cost them a heavy tax for many years.)

Jewish university graduates could apply for permission to live outside the Pale and to hold government posts. Later, in 1879, this privilege was extended to Jewish pharmacists, dentists, male nurses, and midwives. The government debated for almost ten years what to do about the Jewish artisans. Finally, Alexander decreed that artisans, mechanics, distillers, and artisans' apprentices could settle throughout the empire. But so many restrictions and qualifications were added that this opened only the smallest hole in the great ghetto wall. Few artisans managed to get out. It was rather the traders, disguised as artisans, who slipped through into the interior, where competition was less fierce. To stay out of jail they bribed the police. When caught, they were exiled.

Casting about for other ways to Russify the Jews, Alexander II revived the idea of abolishing the centuries-old institution of the cheder and the melamed. In 1855 it was decreed that within twenty years all teachers or rabbis must be graduates of a government-run rabbinical seminary or institution of higher learning. But the cheders and the melamdim went on in their accustomed way, resisting every attempt to change them. In 1873 the government gave up the idea of closing the cheder. Instead, it closed the two seminaries and the hundred state schools that were supposed to remake all Jews into Russians.

It was but another example of the puzzling maze of regulations covering the Jews. Visitors to nineteenth-century Russia could rarely understand them. "This, however, is not surprising," wrote Francis Palmer, an Englishman who managed large estates in Russia. The regulations, he said, "can hardly be understood in Russia itself, in consequence of the system by which new regulations and edicts are frequently issued by the Government without revoking others—sometimes of quite a contradictory nature—already in force. The result is that the new edict is often found to be altogether unworkable, but instead of being recalled, it is allowed to remain while yet another is added. The consequence of this is that the local administrations, while carrying out the intentions of the Government in their general principles, do not really execute the actual letter of the law."

# 6 I WAS, WITH GOD'S HELP, A POOR MAN

LIKE MILLIONS OF OTHER EASTERN EUropean Jews, Selman Waksman was raised in a shtetl. The shtetls—the word means small town—were essentially marketplaces, the regional centers for trading goods and services. They were country towns made up of innkeepers and distillers, peddlers and artisans, shopkeepers and wholesalers. Not to mention the *luftmenschen*, the people "living on air"—beggars, hangers-on, dreamers. The shtetl's population might be largely Jewish, wholly Jewish, or mixed, with a strong Jewish minority.

Selman Waksman was born in Novaia-Priluka, a town in the Russian Ukraine. It had been the birthplace of his mother and of her mother too. Selman, who grew up to become a microbiologist and a Nobel prize winner, never forgot what Novaia-Priluka was like:

> *It was a bleak town, a mere dot on the boundless steppes. It was flat and surrounded by wide, forestless acres. In summer, the fields of wheat, rye, barley, and*

*oats formed an endless sea. In winter, snow covered the ground, and the frosted rivers carried the eye to the boundless horizon, where the skies met the earth somewhere far away. Only the slow-flowing rivers and brooks, with occasional groves of oak and chestnut, broke this continuity of land and sky. The earth was black . . .*

*It was a small town. Very few of its inhabitants obtained from life more than a bleak existence, and even that required hard, continuous struggle. In spite of the abundant crops and the well-fed herds of cattle and sheep, of swine and horses, and the hard-working people, life was materially poor, since the resources went to fill the coffers of the landlords, the Czar and his retinue, and the police . . .*

*Many of the houses in town were attached to one another, in rows of fifteen or twenty . . . Most of the houses consisted of a large living room with a lime-washed earthen floor, a small bedroom, and usually a small kitchen, the major part of which was occupied by a thick-walled clay stove. This stove served many important functions: for baking the weekly supply of bread, for preparing the daily meals, for heating the house, and occasionally offering extra sleeping quarters for guests or members of the family. Its broad, flat, clay-coated surface could often be offered, especially in winter, as a welcome resting place to the visitor or to the youngsters of the family. Occasionally, the house had a cellar or garret, both serving to enlarge the living quarters of the household or to provide extra storage space for casks of pickled vegetables, fruits and home-made beverages.*

*Here and there on the outskirts of the town was a house somewhat more impressive than the others. A tin-covered roof, a slightly larger structure containing more than the usual three rooms, a wooden fence, and often an adjoining small garden were the meager niceties that indicated the wealthier inhabitants . . .*

*Several parallel rows of whitewashed, straw-thatched adobe houses surrounded a large open square, with a well at one corner. Here, on religious festivals or on market days, the peasants from various villages would come to trade, to sell their agricultural produce, and to buy manufactured goods. They also came to meet friends and to make merry. Returning to their villages in their creaky, ungreased, horse- or ox-drawn wagons in summer, and in their smooth-running sleighs in winter, they left the square full of garbage and refuse. Then for several days, peasant women cleaned up the debris with their longhandled brooms made of reeds and rushes growing close to the local brook, and again the square was bare.*

There was always such a market square in the towns of the Pale. Michael Charnofsky pictures his Warshilovka:

*The center of the town had one square block of stores built of brick, about ten stores on each side. The four corners had the biggest stores and the others were smaller sizes for shoemakers, for capmakers or tailors, or novelties and other small businesses. But the corner stores were the big businesses. One was a big hardware store, the second a big grocery, the third sold yard goods, and the fourth farm implements.*

Every other Sunday was *yarid* (market) day at Warshilovka. Hundreds of peasants would come from the surrounding villages and farms to trade:

*They would first go to church, and that part would be jammed with people. The main attraction was the numerous beggars. Two lines formed. Between the lines walking to the gate the beggars would sing religious songs and the people would give them money . . . On the yarid day the streets would all be filled with different articles and livestock. On one street there would be wagons all laden with oats, hay, wheat, corn and buckwheat; another street (called* Lebediga-Gasse, *the Life Street) would be all cows, sheep, goats, pigs, and horses. The other streets had amusements in tents. The main business was done around the stores.*

The great majority of Russia's Jews lived in such towns, scattered in the thousands over the Pale of Settlement. Of the 7 million Jews in Eastern Europe toward the end of the nineteenth century, about 5 million lived under the czar. The rest were next door in Rumania, Hungary, and Austro-Hungarian Galicia.

The Pale of Settlement, which ran about a thousand

miles in length and three hundred miles across, corresponded roughly to what are now the Soviet republics of Lithuania, Byelorussia, the Ukraine, and the eastern part of today's Poland.

While the Jews were only about 5 percent of Russia's population, they made up perhaps a fourth of the people who lived in the towns. In contrast with the Jews, only a small portion of the other people of Russia lived in or near enough to towns to be affected by urban life. Francis Palmer observed that about four out of every five Russians lived in regions "that modern life and thought as yet hardly touched to any appreciable extent."

The towns were islands in a sea of poor, illiterate peasants. But were the people in the towns any better off? Take the town in White Russia that Morris R. Cohen had lived in as a boy in the 1880's:

> Anyone accustomed to the American standard of living who might have come to Neshwies in those days and walked through its unpaved and unlighted streets, looked into its small, unventilated and often overcrowded wooden houses, devoid of all plumbing or the simplest precautions against contagious diseases of an epidemic character, would have pronounced the town unbelievably poor, dirty, criminally ignorant as to hygiene and altogether lifeless. Indeed, he would have wondered how its six to eight thousand inhabitants managed to live at all . . .
>
> About the dirt and material poverty of the town there could be no doubt. It was miles from the nearest

*railway station. There were no factories or large industries to sustain its economy. So far as anyone could tell, the town lived on trade with the peasants who brought to its markets their wood, potatoes and grain and took back salt, nails, kerosene, and sometimes linen goods, shoes and other "luxuries," besides a little money to help pay their taxes. The stationing of a cavalry regiment must have added to the commerce of the town, though the military supplies came in wagons from the outside world, and the officers and soldiers did not seem to have very much money to spend.*

*A very serious handicap was the meager water supply from the few wells. There was a pond at the outskirts of the town. But as the stables of the cavalry regiment bordered on it, people did well not to drink its water, except after boiling. They supplemented the amount they bought from water-carriers by gathering in the rain in simple, primitive ways. Thus, every time it rained, pots and pails were put out to catch the water that came over the massive buttresses of the military barracks.*

*This lack of water made people helpless against the frequent fires which in the summer would sweep away many houses—none of them insured. I remember that every time the weekly portion of the Pentateuch began with Numbers, chapter 9, "Thou shalt kindle," we expected a fire. In one of these, the young son of a former neighbor of ours and his blind grandfather whom he was leading through a street were caught and burnt to death. When such fires broke out we used to pack up our belongings in a few bundles, carry them to a nearby field, and wait between hope and fear . . .*

A town "renowned for its poverty" was Slutzk, in the province of Minsk. "My grandparents spent their whole life fending off poverty," wrote Ephraim E. Lisitzky, "but poverty refused to desert its old friends. This house of theirs, with its clay floor, mildewy and spider-webbed walls, its sooty ceilings, dripping filth whenever the oven was lit—where could poverty find a finer residence?"

Poverty—the word is repeated again and again in the memoirs of shtetl dwellers. Samuel Schwartz, who came from Nagyzöllös in Austro-Hungary, puts it this way:

*When I say poverty I mean a situation such as is hardly thinkable in our land of plenty [America]. It was nothing unusual to have been occasionally without bread in the house. To obtain it, we either had to borrow a slice from a neighbor or buy a loaf on credit. It often happened that there was not a match in the house to kindle a stove or light the petroleum lamp, if there was wood in the stove or kerosene in the lamp . . .*

*Most of the time our home consisted of one or one-and-a-half rooms and kitchen. The latter was shared most of the time with another tenant. If you ask how we managed—well, we just managed; even if I told you, you would not understand . . . Our food was sparse and simple . . . We often did not have*

*enough wooden spoons with which to consume it
when we were all together. Our bread was made of
coarse corn meal, not the fancy corn bread we know
here as a delicacy, but a huge coarse loaf . . . A piece
of white bread was a rare treat. Potatoes, beans and
other vegetables furnished the diet. Milk was a rarity,
as were eggs. Meat was only for* Shabbos . . .

Israel Wolwolff, who lived in Mitterkiefke, recalls
that even with everyone in the family working—father,
mother, children—all they could manage for food was
bread and vegetable soup, "and for Friday—the big
day—a soup made of meat and bones, which father
would bring home especially for the Sabbath meal." The
*kugel* and *challah* his mother prepared especially for the
Sabbath were foods they did not taste all week long.

The most common diet was potatoes and herring.
Sometimes not even herring was possible, and poor Jews
lived on bread and potatoes. "My parents didn't actually
starve," said one Jew, "but were always on the brim of
starvation."

There were plenty of Jews who did starve. The Englishman Sir Moses Montefiore, touring Russia in 1846,
wrote in his diary that he had never seen such poverty as
among these Jews. At Willcomin, near Vilna, he said he
learned that in the previous year one Jew out of four had
died of hunger. Tevye, the dairyman created by Sholem
Aleichem, says, "I was, with God's help, a poor man." In
the shtetl the Jews "may not take their poverty to
heart," said Maurice Samuel, "but they are aware of it; it

fills the house, it is the continuous undertone in their lives, it lurks in all the conversations of the grown-ups. It is a presence and a personality—*dallus*, poverty—referred to with a sort of affection, born of long familiarity . . ."

The homes of the peasants, who lived close by the Jews in the small shtetls or on the outskirts of the larger ones, often looked better. In *Life Is with People*, the classic study of the Jewish small towns of Eastern Europe, Mark Zborowski and Elizabeth Herzog offer this explanation:

> *The poorest peasant spends his spare time puttering about his home, repairing the door, the fence, the whitewashed walls. The impoverished city dweller accepts the condition of his home as part of the state of things, beyond his jurisdiction.*
>
> *The general appearance of neglect declares in addition the fact that the house is viewed as a temporary shell. "My shtetl" is the people who live in it, not the place or the buildings or the street. "My home" is the family and family activities, not the walls or the yard or the broken-down fence. A shtetl family that has lived in the same house for generations would detest and resist the idea of moving away. Yet, essentially, the house remains a temporary dwelling, inhabited for a brief moment of history. It is not part of the family entity, to be cherished and tended. Doctrine teaches that only the mind and the spirit endure—"life is a hallway to heaven"—and even the least soulful Jews*

*of the shtetl, through force of circumstances if not of conviction, treat their physical dwelling places in accordance with this teaching.*

*A long history of exile and eviction strengthens the tendency to regard the dwelling place as a husk. True, it is not unheard of or even uncommon for a shtetl family to inhabit the same house for a hundred years. Yet at any moment the fatal decree may strike and they may be tossed from the homestead into the deep dust of the road. Daily activities are pursued as if today's condition would continue forever; but the setting in which they are placed is slighted as if it would be snatched away tomorrow.*

The economic life of town and countryside in the Pale were closely interwoven. "But not so the cultural life," says Selman Waksman.

*The inhabitants, the Jews and the Ukrainian peasants, were two distinct peoples, different in racial origins, in historical background, in religion, in habits and customs, in communal life, and even in their very languages. Though they formed an interdependent economic system which dominated the region as a whole, spiritually the two peoples might have lived in different worlds.*

The Jews in the shtetl were an island culture. They lived as a minority within the culture of the majority. That majority conditioned the life of the minority.

Whatever happened to it was bound to have an impact upon the Jews' life. The two groups recognized different values, followed different customs, were often subject to different laws. In a political climate controlled by the czar's innumerable edicts, the people of the shtetl could expect nothing but bad weather.

Living for the most part as a majority in the shtetls, the Jews went on with their own traditional life. They paid little attention to the changing politics of Eastern Europe. What they knew about the non-Jewish world they learned in the course of making a living.

# 7 MAKING A LIVING IN THE SHTETL

HOW DID THE JEWS OF THE SHTETL make a living?

Take Warshilovka, a small town near the city of Vinittsa in the Ukraine. The district was called the breadbasket of Russia; its orchards grew the best fruits; yet poverty was widespread. Warshilovka had only three streets, two hundred Jewish families, and two dozen Gentile families. The town's only industry was a mill where rope was spun out of flax, then made into horse harnesses. The harnesses were shipped to the big cities of the Ukraine.

From Michael Charnofsky, who was brought up in Warshilovka, comes these vignettes of people struggling to make a living there:

> Chaim Laiser was six feet two inches tall; he was thin, with no flesh on his body. His cheekbones stuck out like two horns, a long nose was between them, and his two eyes were sunken, leaving two big holes in the face. Bones, bones all over, pinched with hunger. His wife Sonia was short, only five feet five inches; she was

*thin and lightweight, but on the go all the time—
cleaning, preparing, watching over her family. Moishe,
the eldest son, and Berke, the second son, were just
like the father. Even though they were yet very young
their arms and feet were just like sticks, and their
bodies—you could count every bone, and you won-
dered when they would break in half. The two daughters were not so bad. Their faces were filled out and on
their bodies was some flesh.*

*Chaim Laiser was in the* sichke *business. He had a
machine that cut straw into small, half-inch pieces. He
would fill up big sacks and sell them to people to mix
with the oats to feed their cows, goats and horses. The
machine was located in the center of the barn, with a
long arm to harness the horse to. The horse would
walk in a circle around the machine and turn the
knives that cut the straw. In one day he cut enough
sichke to supply all his customers who couldn't afford
pure oats and had to fool their cows, goats and horses
by mixing oats with sichke. With what he made out of
his business he was able to buy one pood of flour, to
bake bread for the family for the week.*

Because Laiser had no pasture for his horse and
couldn't afford to feed him all week for the one day's
work, he arranged with Noah the water carrier to let him
use the horse the other days of the week in return for
feeding it. At harvest time Laiser helped peasants in
return for potatoes, onions, eggs, and a chicken for the
Sabbath. In the winter Charnofsky's father gave Laiser a

few weeks' work. With his pay Laiser bought kindling wood, without which his family would have frozen to death.

At Passover time the village women brought him the dough they had rolled because he had a big oven. He baked it into *matzos* for them, getting enough money to make matzos for his own family.

When the orchards ripened, Laiser worked from early morning until nightfall, picking fruit for half a ruble a day. In two months he went from cherries to plums, pears, and apples. That was his "prosperous" season. When fall came, he chopped wood for the townfolk. Charnofsky would hear him say, "A *sach milluches and wainig bruches*." ("Many trades but not much luck.")

Women worked just as hard in Warshilovka. Zelda Baron was a widow left with eight children, the oldest only twelve and the youngest three. She had to make a living for them all. She got up before daybreak and by the kerosene lamplight woke each child in turn, washed it, dressed it, and served them all breakfast. She had a cow of her own; it gave her milk and she thanked God for it every time she fed the children.

When the sun was up and the people came out to do business, she tended to her own. She had a basement rented from a store on the square and she kept fruit there, bringing it out to a stand on the street each morning. Her two oldest boys helped her.

When yarid came—it was twice a month, on the second and fourth Sundays—the streets were jammed, and there was competition from the peasants who brought their own fruit to sell. Zelda sat all eight of her children behind her fruit stand and appealed to the crowds to buy her fruit. "I must support my eight children; my husband is dead. Buying my fruit will help me. The children must eat." She repeated it all day long, and it worked. She bought food with what she earned and twice a week baked bread and cooked the potatoes and beans needed for the next few days. For the Sabbath she prepared a big lung and liver the butcher would save for her because he knew she couldn't afford choicer meat. Her children didn't starve but they were always hungry.

Moisha Zadels made his living as the town usurer, lending money to Jew or Gentile. He made loans only on articles the borrower brought him: copper or brass utensils, clothing, watches, rings, pillows, featherbeds, quilts, blankets, whatever. He set the price for each article and there was no arguing with him. "If he loaned ten rubles he would take two rubles off for the interest and give you only eight rubles to pay back in ten months, one ruble a month. On the last payment he would return the article."

Most of the town's Jews and many of the peasants were in hock to him. He was strict: fail to pay and you were hit with double interest. If you still didn't come up with the money, you lost your article. About twice a year he would load his wagon with such articles and sell them in Vinittsa.

Moisha was miserly: he never gave to charity and but little to the synagogue. No one liked him, everyone avoided him. In the synagogue no one would sit next to him. He was never called to the Torah, never given an honor. He didn't seem to care.

He got his reward when his house burned down one cold winter night. He lost all his own cash and property, and the fire consumed all the articles people had pawned. The borrowers stopped paying because he had nothing to return to them. Moisha and his family became one of the many poor families of Warshilovka.

There were water carriers in every town. Ephraim Lisitzky remembered seeing his father at the trade.

*From early morning till late at night he shuffled along the streets and alleys of Minsk, loaded down with his yoke and two pails, going from house to house, carrying water for a paltry fee. In the summer he would come home late at night, blistered from the sun and soaking with sweat; in the fall he would be drenched from head to foot; and in the winter he would appear at the table frozen, rime-bearded, and coated with ice. He would sit down, miserably fatigued, and groan through supper. He would fall asleep over the grace after meals, his head slumping on the table, the last word of the grace crumbling from his lips.*

*My father had been a yeshiva student in his youth. Necessity had forced him to become a water-carrier, but he had never become reconciled to his lot . . . Sometimes, on the way to or from cheder, I would see my father coming toward me, the yoke across his shoulders. His face would redden with humiliation, and he would turn into the nearest courtyard . . .*

Uncle Reuben, another of Lisitzky's family, was an itinerant tailor.

> He walked from village to village sewing shortcoats, trousers, and other clothing for peasant families. Every Sunday he would put a small, hand-operated sewing machine on one shoulder, and a bag on the other shoulder with the rest of his sewing implements, bread for the week and, of course, prayer shawl, phylacteries, and prayer book. Thus loaded, he would set out on his rounds of the farms.
>
> When he had a job to do for a peasant, he would settle down in the farmhouse, eating the bread he had brought along from home together with the potatoes the peasant wife baked in the hearth. He would share the peasant's bed of boards, which served for the whole family. The peasants were fond of Uncle Reuben. He never cheated them, his prices were reasonable, and he never kept for himself the leftovers from the material they supplied him with. And during his visit he regaled them with news of the great world and edifying stories from the holy books. He was treated as an honored guest. When Uncle Reuben was ready to leave, the peasants would give him bunches of onions and garlic, bags of beans and peas and millet and spilt, and similar country gifts. For his part, Uncle Reuben liked the peasants, too. He spent most of his time in their households, and felt like one of the family.

The mother of Israel Wolwolff was one of the countless women in the Pale who labored endlessly to help support the family. His father sold glass and sieves, and with horse and wagon would travel from village to village, returning Friday afternoon for the Sabbath after having earned $1.50 or $2.00 during the week. Israel recalls how one day . . .

> . . . *a wagon arrived with a sack of flour weighing 200 pounds. This proved the beginning of the knish-baking business for mother. She started immediately to bake knishes to be sold—in that way hoping to contribute to the family larder. At this time of my life I was attending public school, and after school hours I used to help my mother, who had a stand where she sold her knishes. I would come to relieve her so that she could go home and make more of her wares. Towards evening, when the day's business was over, and all my knishes were sold, I would go home also. In the evening my mother would knead the flour and prepare the dough for the next morning. At dawn she would fill the squares of dough with potatoes and buckwheat, and then bake them in the oven. By morning the knishes were all ready for marketing.*

Israel's young mind was alert for other ways to help his father and mother. He bought matches wholesale from a village store and paid a peasant ten kopeks to take him with him when he drove the seven miles to another village for the market held on alternate Sundays. He had to rise early enough to get to the market two hours before dawn, when buying and selling began. He would put a rope around a case of matches, tie it to his shoulder, and drag the case through the aisles between the merchants and farmers, crying, "Who will buy my matches?"

When the day's business ended at two in the afternoon, he rode back home. After counting all his expenses, he found his profit was about $1.50. "When I came home in the evening I would give my mother $1.00 and keep the remainder for myself. With this I would buy a top or marbles, and sometimes candy. I was then a grown man of eight years."

He sold matches for six months, then rock salt for another six months, till adults complained the child was undercutting them. He kept on trying. Next it was rabbit skins, then a smoked, dried fish which came in bales. Now he had an assistant, his seven-year-old brother Hyman. All the while he continued to help his mother sell knishes on weekdays, for his own merchandising was limited to Sundays. He drove calves for a cattle dealer, once chasing them three hours through a rainstorm over a distance of seven miles. He did odd jobs for the owner of a dress-goods store close by his mother's knish stand, and by the time he was eleven, the owner was taking him along on business trips to the big market in Karillov, one hundred miles off. "At home I was an important person. I had money to do with as I pleased and could give it to whom I pleased—a big man of eleven years!" But he began to realize what little future there was in this buying and selling to keep your head barely above poverty. One day he would manage to get to America.

Simche and Molke were another couple who had a hard time in Warshilovka. Molke explained to her three biggest children that they must help earn some money; their father couldn't do it alone. She learned to make *kvass*, an iced punch sweetened with saccharine and colored a bright red. They would sell it to the peasants at the biweekly yarid during the hot summer months. She poured the drink into three big tubs, covering the tops with a white sheet, leaving an opening to fill the glasses. Then she put a board across each top to display the drinking glasses. The family was ready for business:

> *Chaim, Fishel, and Mailech, nine, eight and seven years old, were at their post selling kwass. They learned to call out loudly, "Kwass, kwass! Drink kwass!" And their business went better every time. Once when Molke's brother was in town and heard the boys sell their kwass he thought of a new way, even more appealing, to call out. "Kwass frontzsky he govoreet po Russkie kwass kwasok Kwassachock chto kwass piea tho shunke no biea." This meant: "French kwass that speaks Russian. He who drinks this kwass doesn't beat his wife." The peasants loved this song and at times they gathered around the place listening to them call out about the kwass. This really worked up the business, until the boys brought home close to two dollars each and Molke could afford to buy meat twice a week and cook a wonderful dinner for all . . .*

*Life Is with People* gives the flavor of the shtetl's marketplace:

*Bargaining is raised to a fine art. For Jew and peas-*
*ant alike, to pay the price asked or to refuse to modify*
*the first price named would be contrary to custom. If*
*it is an important negotiation between men, like the*
*sale of a cow or a horse, the ceremonial of transaction*
*involves the stretching out and withdrawing of hands,*
*the seller striking his palm against the palm of the*
*buyer, the buyer pulling away until agreement is*
*reached when they shake hands and thus seal the*
*bargain.*

*When the buyer or seller is a woman, which is often*
*the case, the procedure is more verbal and much more*
*vivacious. The acquisition of a Sabbath fish may take*
*on all the suspense of a pitched battle, with onlookers*
*cheering and participants thoroughly enjoying the*
*mutual barrage of insults and exhortations. Points are*
*scored through technique and finesse, and the process*
*of bargaining has as much interest and zest as the final*
*result . . .*

The marketplace was where Jew and non-Jew came
together. The non-Jew was the farmer. The Jew, offi-
cially barred from owning farmland, was the town
dweller. Apart from meeting in the market and at scattered business negotiations, they lived in different
worlds.

Business was usually done in a friendly way.

*The peasant will have his special peddler for small*
*purchases, his special customer for eggs or potatoes.*
*He will give first preference to this Jew, loyally repuls-*

*ing other offers. The Jew will try to buy his grain regularly of one peasant. A sturdy business relationship is built up between them. At the same time, each distrusts and fears the other. It is not that each knows the other will try to cheat him in bargaining, for this is merely a part of the market game, a game that belongs to Eastern Europe and is as native to the peasant as to the Jew . . .*

Beneath the surface dealing there lay a sense of difference and danger.

The market square in Poniewierz, Lithuania
*YIVO Institute for Jewish Research*

*Secretly each feels superior to the other, the Jew in intellect and spirit, the "goy" in physical force—his own and that of his group. By the same token each feels at a disadvantage opposite the other, the peasant uneasy at the intellectuality he attributes to the Jew, the Jew oppressed by the physical power he attributes to the goy . . .*

The Jews sometimes had to flout regulations to make a living. A license was needed to sell certain things and people often didn't have one. What might happen then? *Life Is with People* tells:

*Illegal selling of bagel is viewed as a respectable way for an "orphan" to help his widowed mother. When she has baked a fresh batch of the crusty, ring-shaped rolls, her six- and seven-year-old sons will take them out to hawk on the streets, packed in a basket covered with a piece of clean linen. They will sell as many as they can to anyone lucky enough to have a penny. Suddenly the alarm will be sounded in a whisper, "The 'sixer' (policeman)!" At once the children will disappear from the street; no one has seen or heard of them. Half-eaten bagel will suddenly be shoved into pockets or market bags. When the "sixer" is well out of the way the frightened boys will peek out to be reassured, and perhaps consoled by a sweet from some sympathetic passer-by. Everyone knows that if they were caught they would be beaten, and their baskets would be taken away with the bagel—of which the constabulary is very fond—and the precious linen cover. That they are guilty of selling without a license is a matter of concern to the government, but certainly not to their customers or to those who only wish they had a penny for a piping-hot roll.. . .*

Ephraim Lisitzky's grandparents both worked to support their nine children. Six of them were girls who came to the marrying age one right after another. The dowry drain must have been unbearable. Grandfather drove a dilapidated droshky harnessed to a skinny nag, and passengers took him only if no other droshky was in sight. What his grandmother did to help out, Ephraim could not forget:

*Summers, she hired out to work in the vegetable gardens on the outskirts of Slutzk alongside other poor women. She left at sunrise and spent all day spading, furrowing, weeding, and picking. She returned home at sunset, her back bent, her whole body aching and gritty. Home, she would cut up some cucumbers and onions, toss the slices into a cucumber brine whitened with buttermilk, and serve the dish with dry black bread. Sitting down to eat with the family, she would rest her weary head on her arm and fall asleep, forgetting all about her hunger.*

*In the winter, Grandmother sold potatoes, frozen apples and pears, chickens, geese and similar commodities. She stayed in the market all day. When she came home her dress was frozen stiff, her body a piece of solid ice. Thawing out at the oven, she set a pot of water on the fire, threw in some slices of potatoes, groats, and onion, sprinkled on salt and pepper, and prepared the famous Slutzk krupnik . . . After supper, she cleared the dishes from the table to make room for the pile of feathers from the fowls she had accepted to pluck for a few pennies. She plucked until midnight. Every now and then she would doze off, her head nodding—but her fingers miraculously worked of their own accord.*

*Between Purim and Passover Grandmother worked in a matzo bakery. Every day during that period she stood over the dough crib from dawn until midnight, kneading dough. Two days before Passover she returned home, her hands as puffed up as the dough she had kneaded, her back so twisted she could hardly straighten up without cracking her bones. Groaning, she cleaned the house, made the utensils kosher for Passover, and prepared meals. The first night of Passover, Grandmother's groans mingled with Grandfather's sad chanting of the Passover Haggadah at the seder.*

Reb Eliahu and Reb Shloime were two men Zalman Shazar singled out in the little town of Steibtz, where he came from. They were the *shochtim,* ritual slaughterers:

*Though for decades, both in the slaughterhouse outside the town and in their own courtyards, they had slaughtered cattle for the butchers and fowl for the housewives and heard the cows groaning and seen the chickens writhing at their feet and flashed their rigorously sharpened knives and stained their long coats with blood—for all that, strangely enough, the two of them were the kindest of men and so gentle that they seemed incapable of hurting a fly.*

*Reb Eliahu was the veteran shochet of the two, but he was much more than a shochet. The town wits used to say that he had so many occupations you could people a whole community with him. Besides being a slaughterer, he was the reader in the Old Synagogue, he blew the* shofar on the High Holy Days, *he was the chief* mohel *performing circumcisions in the town, and he was renowned as a matchmaker, having good connections with the best matchmakers in the country and serving all the wealthy families of the vicinity. He took the place of a Government-appointed rabbi, keeping a register of births and arranging certificates. In addition to all this, he spent hours every day cutting gravestones and carving ornamental designs on them: hands lifted in blessing in the case of a member of the priestly class; pitchers of water for libation in the case of a Levite; chopped-down trees to indicate young lives that had been prematurely ended. And he carved rhymed eulogies in verse of his own composition on the stones: the Hebrew was most elegant and the letters at the beginning of the lines gave you the names of the dead.*

*He had still another truly unique occupation—nowadays we would say he operated an employment agency for rabbis . . . Clearly, Reb Eliahu's sources of income were many; some hard, some easy, some conventional, some unconventional. But the end result of them all was that he had the greatest difficulty in providing for his wife, his sons and daughters and sons-in-law and their children. All his long life he was a poor man. But he was a very dignified and serene poor man, a wise and gentle one . . .*

Steibtz was a simple town, not distinguished for its learning or its charity. There were dozens of other places, just as ordinary, in the province of Minsk or beyond in the Pale. Yet there was one thing about it that Zalman Shazar wanted everyone to know:

*It was without doubt a center of work—a town of laborers, strong-armed and muscular men. Though Koidenhove had its Hasidic rabbi, it had no river. Though Mir had its renowned yeshiva, it had no railroad. Steibtz had both. It lay on the banks of the River Nieman, which rose at nearby Pesuchna and was covered with rafts floating all the way to mighty Koenigsberg. And a railway line passed through Steibtz on the way from Brisk in Lithuania to Moscow. The noisy, bustling river bank in Steibtz was one of its unique features, too. The entire stretch, from the iron bridge to the ferry over the river, was shaded by trees and covered with parts of boats under construction, rafts ready to be launched, piles of lumber of all sizes and types, heaps of withes used like ropes to bind the rafts.*

*From dawn till the stars came out workers toiled and sweated here. Often after reading conventional discussions of Jewish "parasitism" in the Diaspora, I have found myself wanting to beg the pardon of these long-gone workers of Steibtz whom I knew in my youth. I remember them patching holes in the sides of the boats with rope and fiber; lying on their backs on the ground under larger boats, with huge wooden hammers and long iron files in their hands, closing up cracks from the morning to late hours of the night; hammering away and singing while the breezes blew from the turbulent river. Not all of them were young. There were white-bearded ones, too, with large families, fathers with children and sometimes grandchildren.*

*How horrified the whole town was that ghastly night when the scaffolding snapped and a boat fell on the workers, and Berel Chashe-Breinas was pulled out from underneath crushed to death, still holding a hammer in his hand! And that accusation of parasitism—fruit of the earnest desire to reform the Jewish economic structure—how totally undeserved it was in your case, carpenters and boat builders of Steibtz; planers of boards and fasteners of rafts; carters that worked along with your horses to drag logs from the woods and throw them into the Nieman; transporters of barrels of tar to the boats; loaders and unloaders, tossed by rain and storm and wind during the long, long hours of your working day!*

# 8 THE SHEYNEH
## AND THE PROSTEH

CHAIM LAISER, UNCLE REUBEN, SIMCHE and Molke, Reb Eliahu—they lived by the old saying, "If no bread, then no Torah." The common toast they all knew was *"Gezunt un parnosseh"*—"Health and livelihood." And everybody in the shtetl, of whatever age or sex, pursued *parnosseh*. The scholar too, for study was considered "work for the Creator," and the scholar was busy at it from first light till long after dark.

Those who lived by trading on some scale—the merchants, dealers, storekeepers—took pride in not working with their hands. They considered themselves to be the *sheyneh*, the fine Jews. They were a small minority. The great mass of others were petty middlemen of all sorts, artisans, or unskilled workers.

The widespread impression of the Eastern European Jews as "nonproductive" middlemen isn't borne out by the facts. In the Russian Pale, the Jews were only 4 to 6 percent of the population, but 21 percent of all factory workers were Jews. In Galicia, a fourth of the people working in industry and the crafts were Jews, some two and a half times their share in the general population. There was actually a smaller proportion of Jews engaged

in commerce in Russia than in the countries of Western
Europe. But inside Russia and Galicia most of the
middlemen were Jews. And that fact made it easy to
charge that Jews were nothing but middlemen or, as the
anti-Semites put it, "parasitic peddlers" and "unproductive hucksters."

Ignored was the historical background: that what the
Eastern European Jews did to make a living was restricted by government decrees handed down over hundreds of years. They could not own or operate the
sources of raw materials, they could not travel freely,
they could not live on the land or in large cities. The
effect was to force the majority into the position of
middlemen, buying and selling goods and services.

Ignored too were the considerable number of Jews
who worked with their hands. Some trades became identified with Jews—tailor, cobbler, blacksmith, limeburner.
In some places only Jews were certain kinds of laborers—
teamsters, porters, coachmen, loggers, water carriers.

Few Jews were in agriculture, because the law prevented them from owning farmland. While 90 percent
of the Russians were tilling the soil in the 1870's, less
than 5 percent of the Jews were. The best many could do
was to rent an orchard and hope for a good crop they
could sell to a dealer. The law did not bar Jews from
owning cattle, and dairymen were common in the shtetl.
Some had their own cows. Others bought milk from a
farm and sold it to the shtetl. A lucky few had a horse to
pull the delivery wagon; most had to carry the milk pail
on a shoulder pole, often for miles.

The Jews who did manage to engage in farming had to

do it by leasing the land. Hirsch Abramovitch has described the arrangements made by Jews in the villages of Lithuania. From absentee owners they leased estates ranging from a hundred to several hundred acres, or even more. They paid the rent in advance, generally for six months. Sometimes the terms called for a share of the farm products as well.

The Jewish lessee usually didn't till the soil himself but spent all his time in the field managing the estate. He hired tenant farmers to work for him, giving them huts, groceries, and a patch of land for their own use. Sometimes a sharecropper system was used instead, with the land sublet in return for half the crop. A capable manager did better with his own hired help. The incompetent lessee wound up in bankruptcy.

But even with good management, few Jewish farmers got rich this way. It took the labor of the whole family to make any kind of a living from a leased farm. The women milked the cows, made the cheese and butter, cared for the garden, cooked not only for the family but for the day laborers and the unmarried yearly workers. They also baked the bread, raised the chickens, and watched the ducks. They prepared the feed for the cattle, spun and wove the wool and flax into cloth, and sewed the clothing for the household. And on top of all that, they raised the family, most likely a big one.

The children all helped too, both with the household tasks and the barn and field labor. There was always something that needed doing from dawn until far into the night.

The Jewish farmers raised food, but their families

A country scene in Kovno province, Lithuania
*YIVO Institute for Jewish Research*

didn't eat much of it. *Borsht* was the main dish, eaten twice a day. There was cooked barley, and cereals, and once in a while pancakes. Rarely did they eat meat during the week; that was a Sabbath special, with the meat bought in the town. At the end of the winter, in the calving season, they would have a calf slaughtered, eat some of it, and salt the rest. In late autumn it would be a sheep, and then meat was on the table every day of the week—for a while.

No matter what a Jew did to make a living, it was his *gesheft*, his business, and it was important. But some ways of making a living were esteemed more than others, not only because of the income they brought, but because of the degree of respectability attached to them. It was better to be one's own boss, no matter how shaky the business, than to work for another. Better, too, to be a salesman than a worker. For the salesman used his head, while the worker used only his muscle. In *Life Is with People* the distinction is explained:

> *The shtetl folk feel that "head," kop—and especially "yiddisher kop"—is the chief capital in any enterprise, and sometimes the only one. Yiddisher kop is identified with seykhel, "brains" or "good sense." Every human being has seykhel but "yiddisher seykhel" is of a special kind and quality. It is characterized by rapidity of orientation and grasping of a problem, intuitive perception, and swift application to the situation.*

Such distinctions divided the shtetl socially, partly on the basis of economic position and partly on that of religious status or learning. The artisans in some communities were shunted off to their own synagogue. Within the synagogue people were seated by their social standing. The concept of *yichus*, which had to do with the family's position, again not altogether linked to wealth, contributed to where Jews stood in the community.

The two classes were, from another angle, the intellectual aristocrats and the less learned plebians. In the first class were rabbis, teachers, cantors, students. They spent their time in prayer and study, and looked down upon manual labor as degrading. Fathers felt bad when they had to agree to a son's taking up a trade. They took comfort from recalling what the Gaon had said: that if a man was not fit for pure scholarship, he should be taught a trade and thus enabled to support his more gifted fellow Jews.

The prejudice against working with one's hands was deep-rooted. In his memoirs, the Yiddish poet Eliakum Zunser tells of the humiliations endured by his boyhood friend, Motke Kochel, the son of an innkeeper in Vilna. Motke couldn't study the Talmud for endless hours. He would slip out of the classroom, hide in the attic of the inn, and with wood or clay shape human figures. His father beat him savagely for breaking the divine commandment against the making of graven images. But he would not give up his carving. They fought bitterly over it until at last his father took Motke out of school and apprenticed him to a wood carver. Motke worked for years in the Vilna ghetto, carving what none of his neighbors understood or wanted—until at the age of twenty a government official's wife saw his work, recognized his genius, and sent him to the Imperial Academy of Art in St. Petersburg. He won international renown as the sculptor Mark Antokolsky.

Because he worked with his hands, young Motke was linked in his father's mind with the *prosteh*, the unschooled, the laborers, the artisans, the people destined to do nothing but the dirty work. Yet it was not the occupation itself which brought the negative label but its status in culture and education. If a man who worked with his hands had learning and manners, then he was not prosteh. And the son of prosteh parents could always acquire learning and rise to become one of the sheyneh. Hillel, the great sage, came from a poor family and started life as a water carrier.

The sheyneh thought of the prosteh as loud, violent people, hardly a cut above the crude peasants. The prosteh in turn had their stereotype of the sheyneh, calling them hypocritical pedants who might have a Jewish head but not a Jewish heart. Yes, scholars sat on their behinds and studied day and night, but workers sweated the week long to make the holy Sabbath possible.

But both—the sheyneh and the prosteh—lived by the same code, as *Life Is with People* points out:

> In both groups the dominance of the traditional pattern is accepted in a spirit ranging from affirmation through grumbling to resistance. Proportions differ, and the negative response is higher among the prosteh, yet any prosteh father longs to have a son become a learned man, even though he may swear that scholars are parasites living on the toil of honest fellows like himself . . .
>
> Moreover, while each group harbors a stereotype of the other, each sees the other as an essential partner in the life of the community. One is the man of action, the other the man of thought. The man of learning or of wealth is constant adviser and constant helper. The prosteh not only do the heavy work but in time of

*violence they are strong-armed defenders. And vio-*
*lence is no stranger to the shtetl.*

Because of the nature of their work, the prosteh were in closer touch with the peasants. For them the peasants were the outside world. And by the same token, the outside world saw the shtetl through what they knew of the prosteh. To most Jews in the shtetl, Gentile meant the peasant. And for the peasant, Jew meant the prosteh.

In a portrait of Swislocz, written by one of its sons, Abraham Ain, we get a sense of the economic life of a large shtetl. Swislocz was in the district of Grodno. There were nearly two thousand Jews living there in the 1870's, when the first leather factory was opened. Soon there were eight factories, all owned by Jews, employing forty to fifty workers each, and another dozen or so smaller shops with six to twelve workers.

About 70 percent of the town's Jews made their living from the factories. They were divided into dry and wet tanneries. The leather they produced from horse hides was sold to merchants all over Russia and used to make leggings and uppers for shoes and boots. It took three months to convert a hide into leather. The wet work was mainly unskilled, and most of the workers were non-Jews. The skilled labor of the dry factories was done mostly by Jews. No machinery was used in either type of operation; it was hard work. The lighter labor was done by boys. Most of the town's Jewish boys entered the factories between twelve and fourteen, or were apprenticed to artisans.

Until the early 1900's working conditions in the

leather industry were terrible, Ain wrote. The workers put in a fourteen- or fifteen-hour day, six days a week, and the wages were very low. Not until the *Bund,* the socialist organization of Jewish workers, was formed in 1897 did life improve. Two general strikes in Swislocz made the difference.

There were a hundred Jewish artisans in Swislocz. The largest group were shoemakers (twenty-two), then came tailors (sixteen), bakers (eleven), joiners and black-smiths (nine each), and a scattering of coppersmiths, tinsmiths, bricklayers, glaziers, watchmakers, carpenters, locksmiths, potters, driers, harness-makers, and book-binders. There were several Jews who shifted from one kind of calling to another, doing whatever paid at the moment, and some who were indirectly involved in agriculture on a small scale.

Swislocz had about sixty stores, most of them small. A dozen were run by women whose husbands had other trades. The rest were the sole support of the families owning them. The few big stores catered to the land-owners, the officials, and the leather manufacturers. Until the sale of liquor was made a state monopoly in 1898, there were about a dozen Jewish tavernkeepers. Several Jews dealt in grain, and some were in the timber business. The big timber men hired managers and log-gers; the others did all the work themselves. The better logs were floated down the Narew to the sawmills or to Germany. The others were cut up for railway ties or firewood.

In the town of Bilgoray in Lublin province, where the novelist I. J. Singer was born, the making of sieves was the local industry. These were shipped to all parts of Russia and abroad. In Singer's memoir of his childhood, he tells of the Jewish sievemakers.

*The peasants made sieves only during the otherwise empty winter months, but the several hundred Jewish families in Bilgoray who were engaged in this trade worked at it all year round. The women collected the horse hair from which the sieves were fashioned, then cleaned and washed it. The men sat before the looms like so many spiders trapped between the poles and ropes and did the weaving. It was unhealthy work that caused consumption after twenty years or sooner. Most of the sievemakers worked from before daybreak until well into the night. Bent over their looms, they grew hunchbacked and purblind, their lungs torn from coughing, their faces drained of blood. And their wives wasted away with them.*

*But for all their effort they barely made enough to feed their families. The few wealthy contractors who gave out the work paid next to nothing for the long hours of labor, and it often happened that after a family had slaved for a whole week there was no money left with which to celebrate the Sabbath and they were forced to go begging from door to door. I remember how ashamed they seemed when they came to Grandmother's kitchen. She gave away loaf after loaf of bread, for which they thanked and blessed her. Afterwards, Grandmother railed against the Hasidim who included in their ranks these contractors and some of the worst exploiters and bloodsuckers in town.*

*The street on which the sievemakers lived was a pocket of filth, disease, and poverty, while the contractors grew only fatter and sleeker from day to day.*

There were some Jewish entrepreneurs who reached the heights in Eastern Europe's business world. Pauline Wengeroff, born into such a family of upper-class Jews in 1833, in Bobruisk, White Russia, described them in her memoirs. As a contractor, her father played a great economic role in the first half of the nineteenth century, erecting fortifications for the czar, building roads and canals, and supplying the army. When Pauline married Hanan Wengeroff she went to live in the town of Konotop. "My father-in-law, the richest man in town, held the government's wine and liquor concession. I remember the way the house was furnished—the large rooms, expensive furniture, beautiful silver, carriages and horses, servants, frequent guests."

A little later her husband got the liquor concession in Lubny. In 1859 her husband's father, grandfather, and another partner obtained the leasehold on liquor for the province of Kovno. Her husband was put at the head of the office. This was in the early years of the reign of Alexander II, when it was possible, she wrote, "for the Jews to attain an unexpected influence in commerce and industry. Never before or after did the Jews in St. Petersburg live in such wealth and distinction as then, when a good part of the financial affairs of the capital were in their hands. Jewish banking houses were founded. Corporations headed by Jews were organized. The stock exchange and the banks grew to immense proportions."

A few years later the Wengeroffs moved to St. Petersburg.

> *The society we became part of consisted of distinguished and cultivated people, most of whom lived a carefree existence in wealth and luxury.*
>
> *The St. Petersburg Jewish community had a magnificent synagogue and even two rabbis—one modern and seminary-trained, the other Orthodox. But the Jewish community had abandoned many Jewish customs and traditions. The more fashionable even celebrated Christmas. Only Yom Kippur and Passover were observed, but in an up-to-date way. Some Jews drove to the synagogue in their carriages and ate in the intervals between the Yom Kippur service. Passover was kept, even among the most progressive. It remained a festival of remembrance, joyful because it recalled not the exodus from Egypt, but one's own childhood in the shtetl. The seder was observed, in a highly abbreviated form. Even baptized Jews kept the seder. Though they did not themselves make the holiday feast, they welcomed invitations from their not-yet-baptized friends.*
>
> *These were the customs of the upper stratum of Jewish Petersburg. To live in this milieu and remain impervious to it required a strong character and religious fidelity which my husband lacked. Yet here in Petersburg, I had often witnessed the strong feeling of solidarity among these Jews who had given up traditional Judaism. Jews in trouble with the authorities anywhere in Russia used to turn to the Petersburg*

*Jewish community for help. Petersburg Jews spared neither money nor time. They appealed to the highest authorities on behalf of the oppressed Jews. Their concern was natural and understandable. This Jewish solidarity became proverbial all over the world. Even the baptized Jews were not immune to it.*

In 1871 the Wengeroffs moved once more, now to Minsk, where Pauline's husband was made vice director and then director of the Commerce Bank. "Once again we lead a comfortable and prosperous life," she wrote.

A glimpse of another Jewish aristocrat's life comes from a memoir of Baron David Günzburg, written by his daughter Sophie. Baron David, born in Kamenets-Podolski in 1857, belonged to the third generation of a family of financiers. His grandfather Joseph, permitted to settle in Petersburg, founded a bank there bearing his name. The founder's son Horace handled the affairs of the Grand Duke of Hesse-Darmstadt, a high officer of the Russian Army. In gratitude the Duke bestowed the title of baron on Horace and extended it to the entire family.

Horace brought up his sons in a religious and traditional spirit, Sophie said. Her father David, one of the sons, was an intellectual and a noted linguist. He learned a new language almost every year and had mastered thirty-four by the time of his death. He inherited a library of ten thousand volumes and built it to more than fifty thousand, making it one of the largest and finest private collections in the world. Although David was Russia's leading authority on Middle Eastern languages and history, as a Jew he was denied a professorship in the University of St. Petersburg. He opened a school of his own, with the right to confer degrees, and taught most of the subjects himself. He served in two czarist ministries, was active in Jewish community affairs, wrote books and articles, and even gave his children Hebrew lessons every morning at seven.

David, like his father Horace, served the Jews as their friend at the court. Denied so many legal rights, the Jews were forced to depend upon men of influence to get their case before the czar. Such men were called *shtadlanim*, and the Günzburgs were the first to fulfill that role. David, Sophie wrote, "used to intercede with the authorities in crucial matters, thwarting plans (which somehow became known to him) for violence against Jews, freeing an innocent Jew from prison, obtaining residence permits, providing an accused Jew with a fair defense lawyer. He never sought favors for himself . . . Two or three rooms in a small suite [in the Günzburg home] were set aside to house Jews refused residence permits in the capital city. Here they lived in hiding until my father could obtain proper documents for them. They did not leave the house; food was brought into their rooms by our servants."

Jews such as Samuel Solomonovich Poliakov did much to build the railroads that spread across Russia in the 1860's and 1870's. While their enterprise brought them great wealth, the extension of the railroads into the Pale meant a painful readjustment for a great number of other Jews. Jewish innkeepers, drivers, and middlemen of the villages and small towns were deprived of their livelihood and forced to move elsewhere or to change their way of making a living. Zunser wrote a song about their troubles—"*Sogt Kaddish nokh der Velt*" ("Dirge for the World")—in which the coming of the railroad and the telegraph are blamed for bringing about cataclysmic changes in the world they were used to.

# 9 STUDY IS THE
  BEST OF WARES

WHILE LIVING WITH HIS GRAND-
father in Neshwies, young Morris Cohen went
to cheder for six days in every week. The schoolday began
at eight in the morning and ended after six, except for
Friday, when the boys were dismissed a little earlier.
There were few vacation days in the year, only the
holiday weeks of Passover and *Succoth*. Looking back
at his childhood in the old country, Professor Cohen recalled what he learned in cheder:

> *I was taught to translate the Bible into the vernacu-*
> *lar—Yiddish. This was a great joy, especially when we*
> *came to the narrative portions of the Book of Genesis*
> *and later to those of Judges, Samuel, and Kings. These*
> *were my first story books as well as my introduction to*
> *history, and to this day the Biblical stories have an*
> *inexhaustible liveliness for me, as if I had actually*
> *lived through them.*
>
> *My first rebbe in Neshwies was exceedingly poor,*
> *had four children and was very much harassed. In his*
> *irritation, he omitted the usual ritual of deliberate*
> *punishment, the letting down of the trousers and the*

A teacher's assistant taking pupils to cheder somewhere in Eastern Europe. From a Jewish New Year's card of the late nineteenth century

*application of the strap. Instead he lashed out his blows at the least provocation, and sometimes . . . even without provocation . . . The cheder was located on a quiet street, and the long rectangular back yard was covered with grass. I remember especially one late afternoon as the long shadows were fading with the setting sun, I ran around in the yard with a feeling of great elation . . .*

*In the winter, we had to stay in the cheder until after dark and so had to light our way home by carrying lanterns. For a long time the possessing, the cleaning, and the carrying of the lantern, appealed to me as a thrilling adventure. For the rest there were few organized games among us inside or outside of the class-room . . .*

*After two years in my first cheder I was sent to another rebbe, Reb Nehemiah, who was a maskil, that is, one who believed in bringing some of the beauty of Western learning into Hebrew studies. Indeed, he gave private lessons in grammar to advanced pupils who came to his house late in the afternoon or evening . . . But we, the regular pupils, were taught nothing but the traditional curriculum, the Pentateuch with the Commentary of Rashi and a few other books of the Bible. Only in an occasional comment would our rebbe's learning open up for me glimpses of the great outside world of geography and history. I remember particularly his explanation of the origin and evolution of boats and of the Franco-Prussian War of 1870 . . .*

*My mother, who never forgot her disappointment at not having succeeded in her ambition to learn the art of writing, was determined that I should not be similarly handicapped. So she had a letter written to her father that he should see to it that I receive instruction in the art of writing Yiddish. To this my grandfather replied, "My dear daughter, I am giving your son Torah—the substance of life. The trimmings come later."*

In Swislocz, said Abraham Ain, boys of five were sent

to cheder, which was usually in the teacher's home. They were taught the alphabet and reading for the first year and a half, then promoted to a higher grade, where they studied the Pentateuch and the rest of the Bible. The next step was the Talmud. Some teachers also gave the boys writing and arithmetic. By the age of ten, a Jewish boy knew a little of the Bible, could write Yiddish and do some arithmetic, and was studying the Talmud. Some boys were only part-time cheder students and gave several other hours a day to learning Russian, arithmetic, and writing.

Boys whose parents couldn't afford the fee went to a Talmud Torah, where the tuition was low or free. Bible and Talmud classes were mixed with reading, arithmetic, Yiddish, and Russian. Girls did not start their education until seven or eight. They were taught to read and write Hebrew and Yiddish, and to do arithmetic. At the age of thirteen or fourteen they were usually apprenticed to seamstresses. The poorer girls became domestics.

It was not until about 1900 that a general public school, running through the fourth grade, and a modern Hebrew school were opened in Swislocz, for all Jewish children.

This tradition of elementary education—centered on the Bible and Talmud—was almost universal for shtetl Jews. As early as three, and up to thirteen, boys went to school, no matter what their social or economic position. The conviction that Jewish education was for everybody went back to Rashi, the commentator on the Torah and Talmud who lived in the eleventh century. It was Rashi, said Abraham Joshua Heschel, who "democratized Jewish education; he brought the Bible, the *Gemara*, and the *Midrash* to the people, and made the Talmud a popular book, everyman's book . . . Scholarship ceased to be the monopoly of the few and became widely disseminated. In many communities, the untutored became the rare exception."

Uncle Reuben, the itinerant tailor of Slutzk, is an example of this.

*Every day Uncle Reuben awoke before dawn, washed his hands, and recited the daily portion from the Psalms. Later he went to the synagogue where he said the morning prayers and stayed on to study a chapter from the* Mishnah. *On his returning home he would open the thick leather-bound prayer book whose pages had yellowed with age and handling, and recite an additional prayer, comprising excerpts from holy writings, assigned for each day of the week. Then he would eat breakfast, and sit down to work. He sewed, as he prayed, with great dedication; he was meticulously precise, anxious to do credit to his friends, the peasants.*

*At one in the afternoon, Uncle Reuben would stretch out on the sofa, and nap briefly. Then he would wash his hands again, open the Midrash Rabbah, and study the portion of the week. He had a hard time walking the muddy roads of Polesia on his rounds of the villages; but the intricate paths of the Midrash were even harder. En route he would stumble over strange words, lose his way, wander in circles, and finally stop and look desperately around. Where in the world was he! Suddenly, Uncle Reuben's face would light up. "Aha!" He had found his way out of the morass of the Midrash.*

*Back to the synagogue he went for the afternoon prayers, studied The Well of Jacob, said the evening prayers, and listened to the news from the shopkeepers and the young men who read the modern Hebrew papers. After the evening meal he read a chapter from a popular inspirational book using both the original Hebrew and the Yiddish translation in the margins. The women of the household would stop talking at their chores and listen to his loud singsong.*

It is like the shtetl depicted by Mendele Mocher Sforim in one of his stories, "Shloime Red Khayims." He calls it . . .

*a place of learning of old standing, where practically all the inhabitants are scholars, where the House of Study is full of men and youths busily pursuing their studies . . . where, at dusk, between the Minha and the Maariv services, artisans and other simple folk gather around the table to listen to a discourse on the Midrash, the Bible . . . and similar ethical and philosophical works . . .*

Heschel asks:

*What other nation has a lullaby to the effect that "study is the best of wares"? At the birth of a child, the school children come and chant the Shema in*

# UNTER DEM KIND'S VIGELE

LULLABY

Un - ter dem kind's vi - ge - le Shteyt a klor - vays

tsi - ge le. Dos tsi - ge - le z'ge - fo - rn hand - len

Ro - zhin - kes mit mand - len. Ro - zhin - kes mit mand - len

iz zey - er zis, Mayn kind vet zayn ge - zunt___ un frish.___

| | |
|---|---|
| Unter yankele's vigele* | *Under Yankele's cradle* |
| Shteyt a vaysinke tsigele. | *Stands a little white kid.* |
| Tsigele iz geforn handlen | *The little kid went off to trade* |
| Rozhinkes mit mandlen; | *With raisins and almonds;* |
| Dos iz di beste s'choyre, | *These are the best of wares,* |
| Yankele vet lernen toyre. | *Yankele will study the Torah.* |
| Toyre vet er lernen, | *He will study the Torah,* |
| Sforim pet er shraybn, | *He will write learned volumes,* |
| Un a guter un a frumer | *And a good and pious man* |
| Vet er tomid blaybn. | *He will always be.* |

* A variant version, with translation, of the song above.

*unison around the cradle. The child is taken to school of the first time wrapped in a* tallis. *Schoolchildren are referred to as "sacred sheep," and a mother's pet name for her little boy is "mayn tsadikl" (my little saint). Hence, one is ready to sell all household belongings to pay tuition. Women work all their lives to enable their husbands to devote themselves to study. One shares his last morsel of food with a yeshiva* bokher. *And when the melancholy sweet tone of Talmudic study penetrates the poor alleys, exhausted Jews on their pallets are delighted, for they feel they have a share in that study . . . Study was a song of longing, a pouring out of the heart before the Merciful Father, a sort of prayer, a communion and an ardent desire for a purified world.*

The teaching in the cheder used none of the educational methods we call progressive today. The process of learning was endless repetition. The little child had to memorize the strange Hebrew words and their meanings. He learned only the elements of reading and the prayers. Then he advanced to the second cheder, where he studied the *khumesh* (Pentateuch), learning to translate whole sentences and to understand the text. Here he worked with Rashi's commentary, going into interpretation and hidden meanings. In the next stage, the highest cheder, he undertook independent study under the guidance of a teacher more highly qualified than the elementary melamed. Here the study of the Talmud covered all kinds of problems, ancient and modern, religious and secular. The boring mechanical mode the

## OYFN PRIPETSHOK BRENT A FAYERL

Text and Tune
**MARK WARSHAWSKY**

Oy - fn pri - pe - tshok brent a fay - er - l, Un in shtub iz heys.

Un der re - be lern - t kley - ne kind -er - lech dem___ a - leph beyz.

**2.** dem___ a - leph beyz. Zet - zhe kind - er - lech,

Ge-denkt - zhe tay - e - re, Vos ir lern - t do,

Zogt - zhe noch - a - mol un ta - ke noch - a - mol:

**1.** ko - mets a - leph O. **2.** ko - mets a - leph O.

| | |
|---|---|
| Oyfn pripetshok brent a fayerl, <br> Un in shtub iz heys, <br> Un der rebe lernt kleyne kinderlech, <br> Dem aleph-beyz. | *On the hearth a little fire is burning,* <br> *And it is hot in the house,* <br> *And the rebbe's teaching the little children* <br> *The ABC.* |
| *Refrain:* <br>    Zet-zhe kinderlech, <br>       gedenkt-zhe tayere, <br>    Vos ir lernt do: <br>    Zogt-zhe noch amol, un take noch amol, <br>    Komets-aleph: O! | *See now, children,* <br>    *remember, dear ones,* <br>    *What you're learning here:* <br>    *Repeat it over and over again,* <br>    *"A" with a kamets is "O"!* |
| Lernt kinder, mit groys cheyshek, <br> Azoy zog ich aych on; <br> Ver s'vet gicher fun aych kenen ivre, <br> Der bakumt a fon. | *Study, children, with great interest,* <br> *That is what I tell you;* <br> *He who'll know his lessons first* <br> *Will get a banner for a prize.* |

youngster had begun with was now replaced by the true
excitement of learning, when the mind and imagination
are stretched to their full capacity. The boy was ten or
eleven at this point and everyone watched closely to see
if he had the intellectual power to become a Talmudic
scholar. If he did, he was sent on to the highest institution of learning, the rabbinical academy called the
yeshiva.

The old one-room cheder was a "unique juvenile mad-
house," says Maurice Samuel. It was supposed to be the
child's second home, and the melamed a person to be
cherished like one's father. But almost no Jew who has
left a memoir of those early days mentions a rebbe with
affection. Eliakum Zunser describes the bedlam in the
cheder, the scolding, the spanking, the slapping, the
beating with the indispensable *kantchik* (cat-o'-three-
tails). In Sholem Aleichem's stories the boys speak of
their teachers as "the Murderer" or "the Death-Angel."

In his novel, *The Brothers Ashkenazi*, I. J. Singer
etches in acid a melamed in Lodz who taught older
children.

*Reb Boruch Wolf is famous for his cruelty not less
than for his piety and learning. Besides, he overworks
the boys. He holds them in the schoolroom from early
morning till late at night. On Thursday, which is
repetition day, he works with them beyond midnight
and sometimes until the morning hours. He crams
into the children not only the Talmud with all its
accepted commentaries but all kinds of super-
commentaries on the commentaries themselves . . .*

*He wants the boys to learn early how to carry on the heavy burden of Torah and Jewishness.*

*He never teaches the boys the interesting parts of the Talmud, the legends and stories and adventures of the great teachers in Israel. These he considers fit only for women, or for anti-Hasidic Jews, or for others with weak heads . . . He avoids those tractates of the Talmud which deal with bright and cheerful things, like holy days, festivals and jolly customs . . . His learning is as dry and bony and harsh as his own old body. He hates the simple and straightforward, the obvious meaning of a text or interpretation. If it isn't complicated, it isn't learning to him.*

The Yiddish writer I. L. Peretz, who grew up in the 1850's in Zamoscz, a town in Russian Poland, gives a more affectionate picture of his cheder teacher:

*He, too, was small in stature and frail. Though he was an angry little man, quick to fly into a temper, he didn't whip his pupils. His hands would tremble, and he would call to his wife: "Henneh, grab hold of the oven-rake and split the head of the ignoramus!"*

*Henneh, however, remained placidly in her seat near the oven, going on with her plucking of chickens or knitting of socks.*

*But if his angry command had to do with me, she would reply: "Listen, don't you dare touch Leibish! I'll tell Rivele on you!"*

*To eke out a living, Henneh peddled onions and green vegetables from house to house. Rivele, my mother, was one of her customers and the two women were fast friends.*

*"What a wonderful woman Rivele is!" said Henneh. "A female saint. She denies herself and her family necessities in order to give to the poor. And in such amounts! And this murderer wants to hit her Leibishl!"*

*"Nu! Nu!" grumbled the rebbe. "But don't forget to tell her what a rascal he is!"*

Zunser warned young men thinking of becoming melameds:

*May God give you a better profession than teaching; but if, alas, you are doomed to teach, conduct yourselves differently. Little creatures need character training above all. So don't let a child hear oaths and curses, because these will burrow into its head like worms into a young apple. Children are wards entrusted to you, and you are paid by fathers and mothers to guard these wards against harm and to implant into them good habits. If a child sees you behaving badly, if it hears falsehood and deception within your walls, the seeds of corruption enter its soul and the beautiful flower will become a prickly thorn.*

But there was another side to it, Maurice Samuel points out:

*Though children were willing to play tricks on the Rebbi now and then, we never meet with genuine rancour. A Rebbi was looked upon as a natural calamity; it was in the nature of things that he should be impatient, unsympathetic, handy with the kantchik. Children learned to accept his cruelties with something like good humour, and in this they were training themselves for life as Jews. They would have much to put up with from a surrounding world more impatient, more unsympathetic, and handier with the whip than even their Rebbi.*

Samuel asks why the cheder, with its traditional method of teaching that remained the same generation after generation, did not cripple the children's minds. "How is it that they did not become idiots, but on the contrary maintained an astonishingly high level of intelligence and, what is more, actually learned what they were taught?"

He thinks it is because today we tend to exaggerate the sensitivity of children and to underestimate how resilient the human being is at all ages. People endure when they accept the situation, he believes. "The readiness to endure is half the trick of enduring, and those who have not known the better do not lose half their strength whimpering over the worse." Because the children in the Eastern European cheders "took for granted what they had to face in the way of training, they were immune from most of the negative effects."

There was, too, he adds, the important fact that children and parents agreed on the worth of what the cheder was teaching. "Boys were learning in cheder that which their fathers knew and cherished. They were treated as children but they were challenged as adults."

The yeshivas of the nineteenth century drew hundreds of boys from all over Eastern Europe. They were located not in the old centers of learning—Lublin, Cracow, Lemberg—but in the shtetls, the centers of Jewish spiritual life. The yeshiva at Volozhin, the outstanding center of Torah scholarship, was founded in 1802. Others developed in such small towns as Eyshisok, Mir, Slobodka, Telz, Slonim.

Education in the yeshiva rested on independent study, with the teacher used as a guide. The student relied upon himself in his deep analysis of the Talmud. The approach was to examine commentary and interpretation, always moving from the various texts back to the Biblical passages that were their ultimate sources.

The study of the Talmud was called *pilpul*, which is defined in *Life Is with People* as . . .

> *Pepper, and it is as sharp, as spicy, as stimulating as its name implies. It involves comparison of different interpretations, analysis of all possible and impossible aspects of the given problem, and—through an ingenious intellectual combination—the final solution of an apparently insoluble problem.*
>
> *Penetration, scholarship, imagination, memory, logic, wit, subtlety—all are called into play for solving a Talmudic question. The ideal solution is the* khiddush, *an original synthesis that has never before been offered. This mental activity is a delight both to the*

*performer and to his audience. Both enjoy the vigor of the exercise and the adroitness of the accomplishment. And at the same time, both relish demonstrating their ability to perform on so lofty and esoteric a level. When two accomplished scholars engage in pilpul, they will be surrounded by an admiring group that follows each sally in eager silence, and later will discuss the fine points with each other—possibly working up a new argument about which scholar carried the day.*

The yeshiva teacher was respected as much as the rabbi. He was paid not by the parents of the students, as in the cheder, but by the institution. Most of the yeshiva bokhers (yeshiva boys) were the sons of poor parents. The Jewish community undertook to support not only the yeshiva itself, with the salary of its head and the high cost of books, but each student attending it. It was a widespread custom for students to eat in a different house every day of the week. Funds were raised throughout Eastern Europe for these purposes. Every Jew felt obliged to support the study of the law, and the small towns took great pride in their yeshivas.

No degree was given to mark the end of a phase of study. How could you complete study when "the Torah has no bottom?" A diploma was given after a few years in the yeshiva to show that the student had a right to function as a rabbi. He got no scholarly degree or title. A learned man, whether a self-taught cobbler or a yeshiva trained intellectual, was respectfully called Reb, meaning "my teacher." The study of the law never ended. It could be interrupted for a time by circumstances, but the good Jew explored the limitless law as long as he lived, part of his day while working for a living, and all of the day after retirement.

Every shtetl had its men who did nothing but study the Talmud, night and day. The highest honors of the community went to them. They had yichus, they were the "beautiful Jews." If a youth showed promise of being such a scholar, everyone would help provide the opportunity for study. The father would support his son, sisters their brother, a father-in-law his son-in-law. Charnofsky offers a snapshot of such a man in Warshilovka:

> *Zalman Yankew David was a man in his early forties, but he had the appearance of a man in his seventies. Zalman never worked in his life. He was a Talmud student. He always prayed, he always learned, he was almost always at home or in the synagogue. He sat over a* mishnaes, *a* gemura, *a* tillum, *or other such books, reading and studying. He only took time out for eating two meals a day and sleeping and teaching his own three sons the great learning of God, the Talmud, the Torah, and everything that he knew a Jew should learn.*

> *Zalman was well educated. He knew most of the tillim by heart. He could converse with rabbis about the deep Jewish learning, and would show them many interpretations that contradicted the holy books. He could have been a rabbi but had no such desires.*

> *When Zalman married, his wife knew and her father knew that he would never support a family. But*

In a synagogue    *Courtesy Oscar Gruss, New York City*

*his father-in-law wanted him in the family. He said that Zalman was gold and diamonds to a family, so he provided full support for him and his wife.*

*When the father-in-law died, Zalman's wife, Ruth, took over. They already had three children that were growing up, and the needs were big. So she decided to sell* crellin *(beads) to the peasant women at the local* yarids, *and to travel to the nearby* yarids *. . . Ruth worked hard . . . But Ruth was happy. She knew that her husband had to sit at his learning and prayers and that he was shaping and building an afterlife for her and himself and the children. She thought of the* Gan Aden *and of how wonderful it would be there, with no worries, no conflicts, no disagreements, where only people with* treiag mitzvas *(613 good deeds) would be admitted. Her husband would have all of those and would be accepted without a doubt. It was worth all her efforts, all her hard work . . .*

The study of the Talmud has long been considered to be of the highest religious and social value. It is a tradition that goes back to the days of the Second Temple. "Thou shalt study in it day and night" was like a commandment. And Jewish society has always had unlimited admiration for one who followed scholarship as the pathway to God. The sage and the scholar became the aristocrats of the Jewish world. In modern times, that prestige, authority, and position have been accorded by Jews not only to those learned in religious studies but to people of intellectual attainment in secular culture.

# 10 FUN AND FEASTS

THE MOST FUN THE JEWISH CHILDREN OF Warshilovka had came during the winter when the Bug River froze solid. Not that it didn't provide fun in the summertime too. Then they swam in the river. But they couldn't boat on it; that was strictly forbidden by their overcautious parents. The Jewish children watched enviously as the peasants rowed or paddled up and down the stream that flowed through their town.

In the winter, the Bug froze so deep, horse and sleigh crossed the ice without fear of breaking through and people walked across freely. The youngsters turned out for skating. Charnofsky remembered the joy it gave.

*Most of the time we all made our own skates. We took a piece of wood as long as the shoe, put a couple of holes across the width with two strings in to tie to the shoe, and a wire across the length. This made a very good skate, and all we had to do was break it in. When the wire got shiny, the skates were perfect for skating. Our sleds were also homemade. That was easy—even mothers could make sleds for their children. No one ever knew that there were so many children in town until the sleigh-riding came along. Of course the rich children also came out with a servant and a brand-new sled, bought ready-made, or with ready-made skates. We admitted that they had the nicest sleds and skates, but no one was jealous, for we were all out for a good time. The younger children would roam around the market place with their sleds but not for long, because they would get too cold.*

*The bigger children with their skates would go to the Bug. The skating was real exercise, and everyone was warmed up. Everybody was trying his best to outdo the other one. They skated in rings, and they skated holding hands. Then there was a great straight race that went for miles up and back . . . It was at this time that the Gentile and Jewish children would mix, and there were no objections from anyone. In fact, one couldn't tell the difference. They all had red cheeks, sparkling eyes, smiling faces, and sportsman- like feelings—all alike, only some better skaters than others . . . When the full moon was out and re- flected on the white snow and ice, and the frost was mild, our fathers would go out with us, and they too had a good time.*

Play was regarded by the shtetl as a concession, says Maurice Samuel, not a right. He describes what was permitted.

*On Passover you had games of chance with Brazil nuts; on Chanukah you could play cards, or a game resembling "put and take," with little, four-sided spin-*

*ning tops, on which were inscribed letters recalling the miracle of the unspent oil in the Temple in the days of the Maccabees; on the Thirty-third Day of the Omer* (Lag b'Omer, *between Passover and Pentecost*) *there was actually an outing into the fields! On* Purim . . . *there was a play—to be exact, one of two plays, and perhaps even both: the drama of Esther and* The Sale of Joseph.

That joyous day in the fields that took place on Lag b'Omer is described in *Life Is with People.*

> *This is the one day of the year when the boys, with their melamed, go out into the fields and woods to enjoy the outdoor world that otherwise is nonexistent to the cheder. Each brings his lunch in a package, and all the mothers vie to give the best "naseray" and the most savory tidbits, so that they will not "be ashamed" when all the food is opened and pooled in a common meal. The boys play outdoor games, long caftans flapping about their legs, earlocks bobbing as they run and jump, or shoot at a target with bows and arrows. The melamed, who all the year round bars the cheder door against any spirit of play, accepts the antics of this day as part of the approved regime. How happily he accepts it is "something else again" for occasionally it furnishes an opportunity to work off accumulated resentments against the presiding authority of the schoolroom. Excess in this direction is usually checked, however, by the realization that*

*tomorrow the melamed will again reign in his own realm . . .*

Even in cheder the children enjoyed some happy hours. One of them came at twilight, when the melamed went to *shul* (synagogue) for prayers. In winter, the children sat in the darkness (candles were too costly to burn) and, while waiting for their teacher's return, passed the time telling stories.

*Crowding together against the winter cold and the fear of the wonders they are describing, they tell each other tales in which themes carried over from pagan myths jostle with folklore rooted in the Talmud. In the melamed's absence the strict program of Hebrew erudition is broken into by a medley that mingles biblical miracles with the spirits and demons shared by all the folk, Jews and peasants alike. The boys tell each other in turn about the spirits who throng the shul after midnight, and the tricks they play on any-one who has to sleep there—so that a beggar would rather sleep on the floor of the humblest house than enjoy the honor of a bench in the shul. They tell about the devils who haunt the woods at night, the sheydim, and how some of them even get into the shtetl streets when it is very dark. They tell about the dybbuk who enters the soul of a person so that he becomes possessed and speaks with a voice not his own, uttering blasphemies that would be far from his true mind. They tell of Lilith, Adam's first wife, who*

*steals children; and of children kidnapped from their
parents by gypsies, or by wicked men who deliver
them into Army service. Children of Hasidim will
repeat tales their fathers bring from the rebbe's court,
about the miracles wrought by "wonder man."*

Sometimes shtetls had special celebrations. In Shklov,
a village of White Russia on the Dnieper, the Burial
Society—its members were all Hasidim—gave an annual
beanfeast. It was the only reward its members got for a
whole year's hard work—washing the dead and preparing
them for interment, putting on their shrouds, carrying
them to the graveyard, and burying them. In hot
weather or cold, in rain, snow, or ice. The money the
society collected paid for shrouds for the poor, for
upkeep of the cemetery, and for the lone sexton's salary.
What was left went into the beanfeast. It took two days
to prepare it. Zalman Schneour gives this mouth-
watering description of the feast held in the synagogue:

*First, the breaking of bread. For that, each member
of the burial society got a large white roll, and half a
loaf of fresh cornbread. Then to drink each other's
health everyone was given a bottle of brandy. And to
keep it company, a plate of chopped goose-liver, with a
few spoonfuls of freshly melted goose-dripping over it,
as an appetizer.*

*The first course was a slice of carp weighing about a
pound, stuffed, and full of onions and pepper,
trimmed with soft and hard roe, and swimming in
horse-radish, colored and sweetened with beetroot.*

Next, at least a quarter of a fat goose, roasted in its skin, with all the fat on it. And the gizzard and wings, or a stuffed neck and the feet. And to go with it, a big sour cucumber, and a baked apple.

And to raise a thirst, each member of the burial society got a big stack of thin dry toast, with a thick layer of powdered spices on it and pepper and salt, or ginger. This was eaten between courses, munched so loudly that it set the palate on fire, till it had to be quenched with whatever was going in the way of drink, cold beer or dry cider.

After that came a quarter of a pudding, each the size of a big drum, made of noodles, and bound with eggs and goose fat, goose brains, onions and more fat. Each pudding was crisp and brown on the outside, like a walnut, and inside soft and yellow like calves' brains. These puddings were famed all over Shklov. The wealthiest inhabitants never enjoyed anything so rich and tasty. With the pudding went a mountain of pancakes, made with cinnamon and spices. Or dumplings. With fruit in them. Ordinary people would have called them fruit pies. But for the members of the burial society they were just dumplings.

Then the servers brought sacks of winter apples, slung over their shoulders, and handed them round to the guests. Could any of our generation have eaten all that?

Of all festivals the Sabbath was the first. The people of the shtetl worked all week to reach the Sabbath and celebrate it. To them life and religion were inseparable, and the Sabbath was the most beautiful sign of God's grace, of His gift to them. One of Sholem Aleichem's draymen tells what it meant to him:

> When the Sabbath comes I'm a different man, do you hear? I get home betimes on Friday afternoon, and the first thing of course is the baths, if you know what I mean. There I sit on the top row of the steam room and get myself scalded from head to foot. That puts a new skin on me. Fresh as a newborn babe I dance home, and there on the table are the two old brass candlesticks, shining like stars, if you know what I mean, and the two big Sabbath loaves; and there, right beside them, are the winking Sabbath fish, sending out a smell that takes you by the throat. And the house is warm and bright and fresh and clean in every corner. So I sit down like a king, and open the Good Book, and go twice over the week's portion. Then I close the Book, and it's off to the synagogue.
>
> What a homecoming after that! When I open the door and sing out "Good Sabbath" you can hear me at the other end of town. Then comes the benediction by candlelight, and the drop of good old whiskey, that sings right through me, if you know what I mean, and then the Sabbath supper—the shining fish, and the golden soup, and the good old yellow carrots in honey. That night I sleep like a lord, if you know what I mean.
>
> And where am I going in the morning? Why, to the synagogue, of course, as I'm a man and a Jew. And back from the synagogue it's the real Sabbath meal

*again, the grand old chopped radish, and the good old onion, and the jellied calf's foot, if you know what I mean, with a proper smack of garlic. And when you wake up after your Sabbath afternoon nap, and your mouth's dry, and there's a sourness in your belly, if you know what I mean, what's better, I ask you, than a quart or two of cider? Then, when you're good and ready, and fresh and strong, you sit down to the Good Book again, like a giant, and off you go! Chapter after chapter, eh? Psalm after psalm, at the gallop, like the mileposts on the road, if you know what I mean . . .*

Just how the Sabbath was prepared for and enjoyed by such a struggling shtetl family as Simche's and Molke's is depicted in detail in *Jewish Life in the Ukraine.*

*For this holy day Molke would buy thirty pounds of flour to bake challah. She would have dough to take off to make noodles for soup and a kugel, to make poplickes (pancakes) for the children and enough twisted challahs to last through the Sabbath. Then she would get some fish and horseradish, for without fish the Sabbath would lose one custom. Then of course there was meat or, if there was enough money, chicken. She would also have a tzimmes of carrots, and when Simche came home, usually Friday about noon, if he had had a good week and could afford it, he would go out and buy a bottle of wine . . .*

*Molke at sunset would light four candles stuck in candelabra, put on a clean, ironed dress and a silk kerchief on her head, turned in back of her ears. With*

*satisfaction, a sense of accomplishment and devotion,
she would put her hands over the lighted candles,
close her eyes and* bentsh licht *(say her prayers to
open the Sabbath). The children would stay near her,
and it seemed as if a divine spirit filled the room.
When she ended she said, "Good Shabbos" and the
children answer, "Humain" (so it should be).*

*When Simche returned from the synagogue he
would repeat "Good Shabbos" and everybody would
say "Humain." The table was set; the candles threw a
dim light over the room. The white tablecloth glim-
mered and the lights showed two challahs covered
with a hand-embroidered cloth, the bottle of wine and
glasses around it—knives, forks, spoons, all were on
the table. Simche washed his hands, opened the
bottle, filled the bigger glass, put it in the palm of his
hand, and said khiddush, the blessing of God for the
Sabbath. He then took a drink and handed the glass to
Molke. She took a sip and gave each child a sip, beginning with the oldest. Then Simche uncovered the
challah and cut a piece, made a* moitza, *and sat down.*

*Everybody started with the fish, then soup, meat, or
chicken, with kugel made of the noodles, and last the
tzimmes, made of carrots sweetened with sugar. Between the courses Simche and the children would sing
zmiros, a sort of thanksgiving prayer in song. Every
one of the boys tried to be louder than the others and
Molke would sit, her face shining brightly, and help in
the harmonizing. From time to time she would say
humain, and the children would follow suit. As the
candles got low and began to go out only the kerosene*

*lamp was left burning, until Vassil's son, the peasant
friend of the family, would come to turn it out. Molke
would hand him a big piece of challah. No Jew was
allowed to turn out fire on the Sabbath.*

*In total darkness Simche and Molke would sit after
the children were in bed, and talk about the next
world and how a Jew has to prepare for it, how much
good he had to do to his neighbors, to his friends, and
even to his enemies to gain enough mitzvas to go right
to heaven . . .*

*They sat talking until they tired and went to sleep.
And when the Sabbath was gone and the grim week
started, it was again the start of a struggle to make
enough to live on . . .*

The word for week was *vokh,* but it meant more, it
meant everyday life, it meant hard work, it meant the
return from the heavenly joy of the Sabbath to the world
where one was "misunderstood, despised, and often
hated." The people of the shtetl, it was said, lived from
Sabbath to Sabbath, the one day each week that made
all Jews equal and every man a king.

# 11 HASIDISM AND HASKALA

I T WAS ALWAYS *SCHWER ZU SAYN A YID*— hard to be a Jew—in Eastern Europe. To be a Jew meant to face difficulties and dangers every day. Could a Jew escape that condition? Some tried. They had two paths open to them. One was to desert Judaism and convert to another religion. The other was to remain a Jew but to try to change Jewish life so as to eliminate all its difficulties and dangers.

The great mass of Eastern European Jews took neither path. They accepted the challenge of being Jewish and remained loyal. The options nineteenth-century Russia gave them only a small minority accepted. The government let Jews assimilate to the middle class without forcing them to convert to Christianity. And thousands who had the education and the financial means did. In every community the government also imposed, as we have seen, an official Jewish structure to carry out the czar's notions of what the Jews needed. Jews who accepted that structure took their legal problems to secular courts, sent their children to government schools, and looked to the government rabbis for spiritual leadership. But so few embraced this imperial Judaism that it was said Jews on the government payroll exceeded the Jews who acknowledged their authority.

Most of the Jews gave their allegiance to the kahal, despite the czar's attempts to abolish or weaken it. The kahal expressed basic and ancient Jewish concepts of religion and social welfare. It was the outgrowth of Jewish collective life. The government, in trying to destroy it, only succeeded in strengthening it by making membership a courageous and voluntary act. Every Jew who insisted, in defiance of the czar's anger, on remaining within the Jewish collective multiplied the Jewish will to survive. They did not want to assimilate. They cherished their own institutions. They were Jews and they meant to go on living as Jews.

Loyalty to Jewish identity freely given did not mean, however, that there was no conflict within the Jewish community. The old joke, that wherever there are two Jews there are three synagogues, reflects the discord and dissension within the Jewish world.

For many years Eastern European Jewry was divided by the two hostile camps of Hasidism and Haskala. Both, as we have seen, rose in the eighteenth century, Hasidism as a revolutionary movement of religious renewal, the Haskala as the enlightenment. In the beginning, rabbinic Judaism, which for centuries had dominated Eastern European Jewry, felt itself under siege from both camps.

Hasidism, which rapidly won the great majority of shtetl people, seemed the main danger at first. It met violent resistance from the rabbinical scholars and from the sheyneh of the shtetl. The Misnagdim believed Hasidism was such a terrible apostasy that they used denunciation, jailing, and ostracism against it. There was

Hasid and wife. From an early nineteenth-century print
*The New York Public Library Picture Collection*

a time when each group placed marriage with the other on a level with marriage to a non-Jew.

Yet the principles of both were complementary, two aspects of the Jew's relationship to his God, rooted in the same Covenant. The Hasid stressed God's compassion, mercy, and understanding; the Misnagid divine justice and the Jew's obligation to fulfill his duties. By the early nineteenth century, Hasidism and rabbinic Judaism found the boundary lines between them blurred. The Hasids moved from anti-intellectual extremism back to the ancient tradition of respect for learning. They became proud not only of their leaders' magic powers but of their knowledge of the sacred books. The courts of the zaddiks became centers for both the learned and the unlearned, the prosteh and the sheyneh.

While the two movements did not merge, they managed to reconcile their differences. The shtetl world, knowing and needing justice and compassion, rationalism and emotionalism, learning and faith, was able to absorb both movements.

Hasidism was by no means monolithic. There were many variations within the movement, influenced in part by the personalities of the different Hasidic leaders and in part by social and economic differences. *Life Is with People* concludes, however, that the character of the regional divisions of Eastern Europe seemed to have the greatest influence upon patterns of Hasidism.

The Ukrainian Hasids were the prosteh and the uneducated. Their leaders were rarely scholarly, and their followers believed blindly in the magical powers of the zaddikim. The traditional conflict between the rational, scholarly Misnagid and the emotional, untutored Hasid persisted in the Ukraine until the Russian Revolution destroyed that world.

The Lithuanian Jews resisted the Hasidic movement. Known as cool skeptics, the *Litvaks* turned a deaf ear to the ecstatic songs of the Hasidim, and laughed scornfully at the tales of miracle-working rebbes. Nevertheless, says *Life Is with People* . . .

> . . . *little by little, the ethical aspect of the teachings of Besht, the ideals of love for God and Israel, penetrated even into the Lithuanian shtetl and contributed to the formation of a strangely intellectualized Hasidism. Rabbi Zalman Schneour of Lady, 'The Old Rov,' was the founder of this form of rationalistic Hasidism, completely devoid of the magical component and based on three principles: Khokhma, Bina, Death—intelligence, understanding, knowledge. The first letters of the three words from the word Khabad, which is the official name of the movement, although it is also known as the Lubavitsher Hasidism, because the dynasty originated by 'The Old Rov' officiated in the shtetl of Lubavitsh. In Khabad-Hasidism, the mystical relationship of man and his Creator is intellectualized to the maximum and the Hasidic principles of love and compassion toward human beings are based not on emotional sentimentality but on rational principles of ethics and philosophy.*

In the Polish shtetls the zaddik was often a famed

scholar whose following observed every injunction of the *Shulkhan Arukh,* the huge compendium of rabbinical law. The Polish Hasids attended the zaddik's court, but at home they studied the law and saw to it that their children did too, in cheder.

What helped Hasidism and rabbinic Judaism find an accommodation was the common threat they faced in the Haskala. The enlighteners argued that Judaism, like Christianity and Mohammedanism, was a universal religion that was not the possession of a particular people. The Jews in the Diaspora had long ceased to be a people, they held, because a people must live in its own country. There was no longer any nationhood linked to Judaism; rather you were a Frenchman or a German or a Pole "of the Mosaic faith."

From this idea flowed the conviction that Jews should abandon those differences which were not organic with their "universal religion" and insist upon assimilation with the non-Jewish society they lived in, adopting its culture, language, patriotism.

In Western Europe many young followers of the enlightenment swiftly left the Jewish fold altogether. In Eastern Europe the Haskala met strong resistance because of the special national character of Jewish life. The Jews there felt a much greater bond as a distinct people. Their devoted study of Talmud and Cabala, their Hasidism, their economic separation from the Gentile world, their self-government in the kahal, their Yiddish language—all these welded an ancient identity they fought to continue.

The enlighteners tried to batter down Jewish nationalism by claiming that assimilation was inevitable for the Jews; they would be wise to welcome it because it would free Jewry from all its suffering. Anti-Semitism would vanish, they promised, and together with the Gentiles, the Jews would rise to a higher realm of morality and culture.

All through Eastern Europe the early advocates of the enlightenment saw it as a ticket of admission to Gentile society. In Poland, Haskalists criticized traditional Jewish values and customs. They adopted the fashionable Western short jacket, shaved earlocks and beard, and abandoned religious observances. They preferred to be called not Jews but "members of the Polish nation of the Jewish persuasion." They pressured the state to impose reform upon the more stubborn Jews. In Galicia, Joseph II said he would grant the Jews the privilege of religious tolerance, but only if they would become less Jewish, that is, give up the harmful teachings of the Talmud. He started a secular school system for Jewish children with German as the language of instruction. This pleased the Haskalists, who thought German was the natural tongue for Western culture.

In Russia, as we have seen, the small number of prosperous Jews whose activities drew them close to high government circles praised Russian culture. They too, like the Poles, looked to the government to force reform upon Jewish education and religion, and pleaded for the emancipation of such deserving Jews as themselves. Several of these first maskilim converted to Christianity.

Watching these developments in Poland, Galicia, and Russia, the traditionalists and the Hasidim concluded the Haskala was suicidal for Jews. They viewed modernism and secularism as powerful weapons in the hands of enemies. Feeling themselves under siege, they withdrew behind the walls of tradition.

It was the Jews in the larger communities, the centers of trade and commerce and finance, who seized most eagerly upon the new general education. Most of them were literate in Hebrew or Yiddish, and knew as well the local language—German, Polish, Russian, Ukrainian, Lithuanian, or Lettish. They needed education to engage in foreign trade, and their commercial activities pulled them beyond the limits of their own town. Such Jews were among the first to be urbanized when the Eastern European cities were still in their infancy.

The maskils were of many kinds. In Galicia their leading figure was Nachman Krochmal (1785–1840). Faithful to Jewish identity, he used modern scholarship to extend the Jews' intellectual frontiers. The Hebrew press and Hebrew scholarship enjoyed a revival of several decades under maskil influence. In Galicia the merchant-scholars were violently opposed to Hasidism. Joseph Perl went so far as to call in the imperial police to break up Hasidic prayer meetings. On their side, the traditionalists were also guilty of invoking state power against other Jews. When a Russian maskil was on his way to Berlin in pursuit of greater secular knowledge, the traditionalists were said to have got the Prussian government to refuse him a passport because they feared he would desert Judaism while abroad.

To the young Russian and Jewish intellectuals of the mid-nineteenth century the crowning of Alexander II promised liberation from despotism. The Yiddish poet Eliakum Zunser spoke of the czar's early reign as the Golden Epoch of Russian Jewry. He idealized Alexander II, believing in his good will and trusting him to take down all the legal fences that shut the Jews in. Young Jews shared the faith of the Russian intelligentsia in a coming emancipation. They rushed from the Pale to enter the czar's high schools and universities, where they expected to help create a cultural renaissance. The Russian writers who shaped the radical minds of that generation—Chernishevsky, Pisarev, Dobrolyubov—were read avidly by Jewish youth too. The intellectual power that had been dedicated to the study of Talmud turned to the study of science, philosophy, social reform.

"Russification" was the slogan of the day as the government proclaimed its desire to merge the Jews with the "indigenous" population. But how would this be done? Would the Jews achieve·an equality which allowed them their difference? Or would it be an equality that cost them their independent national identity? The czar meant to do it by interfering with the internal life of the Jews. And some maskils went along to the point of allying themselves with government agents to put down the "fanaticism" of the "dark masses" in the shtetls. Rabbis and teachers certified by the state inevitably served the czar's interests and ended up using the police against the Hasidim. They censored Hasidic books and restricted the movement of the zaddikim. The breach widened between the Jewish intellectuals and the Jewish masses, who felt only contempt for those who pushed the czar's assimilation campaign.

The spread of secularism stiffened the resistance of Orthodoxy to all change. The effect upon both rabbinic Judaism and Hasidism was to make them repressive and inflexible. Let a Jew move the slightest distance from the prescribed path and he might be accused of sinning. If he cut his earlocks, if he preferred the shorter coat, if he read a modern book, he was a heretic.

Nevertheless, there was change. Against rabbinic opposition, even the Jewish educational system permitted small innovations. The late nineteenth century saw some secular subjects introduced, and modern teaching methods began to be applied.

The enlighteners built their strongholds at the two ends of the Pale—the ancient city of Vilna in the north and the new metropolis of Odessa in the south. To the port rising on the Black Sea came a group of Jewish merchants from Brod, the Galician town. In the 1820's they started the first school of Jewish general education in Odessa. Lacking traditions, the city became Europeanized before other Jewish communities. Vilna's enlightenment began in the 1830's with two writers who shaped the new Hebrew style—Mordecai Aaron Ginsburg and Abraham Baer Lebensohn. The circle that grew around them was not concerned with assimilation; it struggled to build a solid foundation for the rebirth of Jewish literature.

In the shtetl, as well as in the larger towns, the Haskala made its approach to the learned through the use of Hebrew, "the sacred language." This was the medium the Talmudic scholars used; they would not read Yiddish or the other secular languages. The en-

The weekly Hebrew newspaper of the Haskala. Called *Ha-Melits* (*The Advocate*), it was edited in Odessa by Alexander Zederbaum. It was published for some forty years and served as one of the voices of the Russian Jews. Many of the leading Hebrew writers appeared in its pages

lighteners published newspapers, magazines, books, and pamphlets in Hebrew, with the aim of broadening the horizon of Jewry. The intellectual appeal reached young scholars and some of their elders too.

In *The Brothers Ashkenazi*, I. J. Singer describes Feivel, the ragdealer of Lodz whose passion was rationalism. He spent all his earnings on the literature of the Haskala. Young people gathered secretly in his house to read the "evil books." Pale and terrified students pored over the modernist writings and felt the foundations of their old life dissolving under them. One of Feivel's disciples was thirteen-year-old Nissan, the son of Reb Noske, a teacher of the Talmud. Singer pictures the feverish devotion of young Nissan to the new learning.

*He read day and night, running frequently to Feivel for new material, stealing candles from the synagogue to be able to study when everyone else in the house slept. He read without system whatever Feivel gave him, Mendelssohn's modernist commentary on the Bible, Maimonides's Guide to the Perplexed, German translations which he only half understood, articles in the modernish Hebrew periodical Ha-Shahar, stories and poems and treatises by Smolenskin, Mapu, and Gordon, rationalist essays by Krochmal and Adam Ha-Cohen, fantastic travel books, Hebrew treatises on astronomy and higher mathematics, of which he understood nothing, but which attracted and fascinated him because they represented that great, brilliant, forbidden world which was opposed to everything held sacred by his father. From Mendelssohn he passed on to Solomon Maimon, and from him to Spinoza and Schopenhauer. He mumbled the German words to himself, caught part of their meaning, tried to guess at the rest, lived in a fever of intellectual effort and wild hopes. And with all this he still managed to learn the weekly lesson set by his father . . .*

The Haskala made far deeper inroads upon the cities than the shtetls. But almost no shtetl was without an enlightened soul. True, probably only one, and he spotted by his fellow Jews because he subscribed to a newspaper. Even though they cried shame upon him for reading such ungodly stuff, they pestered him for the news.

Looking back on the Haskala, the writer called the father of Yiddish literature, I. L. Peretz, showed small regard for its accomplishments. In his *Memoirs* he wrote:

> *Enlightenment also signified "education," princi-pally linguistic. For example, "What is the word for 'boots' in all languages?"; a few songs on the theme: "The four seasons of the year"; Fishman's Hebrew grammar; Stern's "Wie haben zie geshlafen?" (How did you sleep?); my officer-teacher of Russian who repeated again and again prechastia, de prechastia (the Russian participle and gerund); the declama-tions: "By the light of the moon" and "I would raise my voice with force, if I would know"; and the fact that Isaac, the only one of my schoolmates who gradu-ated from the gymnasium, was away at that time studying medicine—that was the sum total the En-lightenment contributed to our Jewish way of life!*

In another place, Peretz said:

> *The Enlightenment didn't throw any significant light in any direction. It failed to inspire us with hope, or to provide us with a philosophy that we could live by. Hastily, and without sufficient thought, we leaders took over a foreign formula. The resulting trend was*

*not consonant with the Jewish way of life and thought. It was a misdirection. We didn't know for sure where it meant to go, but certainly it traveled on the wrong road—the wrong road for us Jews!*

Peretz mentioned his fellow townsman Abraham Goldfaden—the first Yiddish dramatist—as "the most hopeful herald" of the enlightenment. Goldfaden thought the Gentile was "panting to greet us and take us in, in one universal brotherhood of man. But, from what we could see in Zamoscz, they hadn't yet stretched out the hand of friendship far enough to be noticed."

With rapid strokes Peretz sketched in the local Polish intelligentsia, with whom the enlightenment leaders thought the Jews should become brothers. One example serves to show Peretz's scorn:

*There's Dr. Skrashinsky, who is good-natured when he's not drunk or in a bad temper because he is not yet drunk. He's an old "intellectual." He, too, has a wife, and three daughters, and they, too, are ugly rather than beautiful. After graduating from medical school and becoming a doctor, he closed his medical books forever, never to open them again. He leaves all medical problems to others. What has happened in the medical profession since he left college, is no concern of his. What he learned there is enough for him. On his rounds in the hospital, he passes rapidly between the rows of beds, casts a glance here and there, asks the patients to stick out their tongues, to turn their heads now to the right, now to the left—and out he goes. The medical aide follows him into the office. There Dr. Skrashinsky hastily and impatiently writes out some 30-odd prescriptions. This is concluded with the ejaculation: "Son of a bitch!" He hands the prescriptions to the assistant, and that's the end of his day's work.*

At least in Zamoscz, he concluded, "the Jews were exhorted by the enlighteners to assimilate with the city riffraff and the backward peasants." As for himself, he added, the enlightenment caused only "a momentary romantic stir in our lives," and then it passed.

# 12 HEBREW—OR YIDDISH?

PERETZ HAD NOTHING GOOD TO SAY FOR
the enlightenment, at least while in one mood. Yet
from the Haskala came a new Jewish literature of which
he himself was a proud part. Poets, novelists, dramatists,
folklorists, historians, journalists created an original
literature out of the treasures of their ancient culture
and the vitality of their contemporary life. An extraor-
dinary feature of this new literature was that it functioned
in two languages—Hebrew and Yiddish.

At the beginning of the literary renaissance, Hebrew
and Yiddish were intense opponents. The early Haskalists despised Yiddish. To them it was the tongue of the
ignorant masses and of the Hasidic courts. Not a language, really, only a jargon. It was like a shameful brand
the long exile had burned into the Jewish people. The
Haskalists revived the ancient Hebrew tongue and used
it to carry on their war against ghetto medievalism and
separatism.

Their enemies, the Hasidists and the Talmudists,
fought bitterly against the spread of modernized Hebrew. To them the sacred tongue was destined for religious study and nothing else. To use it any other way
was an offense, like cutting off the earlocks or shortening
the gaberdine.

Their everyday langauge was Yiddish, the language identified with Sholem Aleichem's Kasrielevky. But the tongue was used far beyond the shtetl. About two thirds of the world's Jews at that time spoke or understood Yiddish. It is a language often described quite misleadingly, says Maurice Samuel, "as an offshoot of Middle High German with an admixture of Hebrew and Slavic. Etymologically nine tenths of the words commonly used in Yiddish are in fact of German origin, but the tone and spirit of the language are as remote from German as the poetry of Burns is from the prose of Milton."

The formation of Yiddish began perhaps a thousand years ago, when Jews from northern France settled along the Rhine and adopted the local German dialects, bending them to their own old speech patterns. The new Yiddish dialect was influenced at once by elements of the Hebrew and Aramaic that were the languages of Jewish religion and scholarship. Slavic tongues too came to modify Yiddish later on, as did the speech of other regions Diaspora Jews lived in. By the sixteenth century Yiddish writing flourished in Italy, where Ashkenazic Jews had settled. A century later Amsterdam Jews were publishing Yiddish books and the first Yiddish newspaper. Not until the mid-nineteenth century, however, would Yiddish literature be more than a vehicle for entertainment and for instructing those shut off from Hebrew, chiefly women and the less literate men.

The pioneer champion of Haskala in Russia was Isaac Baer Levinsohn (1788–1860) of Kremenets. He used the Hebrew language to renew Jewish life, proclaiming the value of manual labor as both a physical and spiritual cure for ghetto Jewry. His book *The House of Judah*, published in 1828 in Vilna, dealt with Jewish life in Russia. The young devoured the message: to seek knowledge, to study not only Hebrew systematically but Russian too, and to learn the skills needed to till the soil.

Nachman Krochmal used Hebrew to examine the Jewish past critically. His *Guide for the Perplexed of the Age* compared Israel's historical path with that of other peoples and found the mark of Jewish individuality to be its absolute spirit, with both faith and reason its essential manifestations. Jewish nationhood was indestructible, he believed, and its unique genius would yet make great contributions. He saw the revival of Hebrew language and literature as the way to develop Judaism's character.

The poets of the Haskala turned to the Bible as a rich literary source, giving new meaning to its lore, applying its humanist values to their own life and times. The kings and prophets, the peasants and shepherds of old Judea, spoke in many a narrative poem to the modern Jews of Eastern Europe. One of the most popular of such writers was Abraham Mapu (1808–67) of Kovno. His historical romances were the first novels in modern Hebrew literature. Implicit in his vision of ancient Palestine, with its Hebrew culture deeply rooted in its own soil, was the contrast with life in the czarist Pale. His intricately plotted love stories, packed with intrigue and adventure, inspired readers with a consciousness of how great and noble Jewish life had been—and could be.

Another Hebrew writer produced by Vilna was Judah Leib Gordon (1830–92). In his epic poems and dramatic monologues he satirized the ugly, stagnant side of Jewish life and attacked the rigid orthodoxy, the ignorance, the bigotry that choked progress and growth. He was not content to worship ancient glories; his aim was to draw upon the best of the old traditions to meet the challenges of modern society.

Like Gordon, Moses Leib Lilienblum (1843–1910) insisted that contemporary society demanded reforms of the Jewish people. His autobiography, *The Sins of Youth*, published in 1876, was one of the most influential books of its time. In his dismal picture of ghetto life in Lithuania, he called for the young to be educated for a useful life. Unless they were, he warned, they would desert the Jewish world. His book was a cry for rabbinic Judaism to recognize the need for inner change, to let outdated customs go, to clear the path for religion to adjust to life.

The Hebrew novelist and editor Peretz Smolenskin (1842–85) came from the Russian province of Mohilev. After a brief stay with Hasidism, he took up secular learning, mastering modern European languages while earning his way as a Hebrew teacher. Refused a permit to publish a Hebrew journal in Russia, he began issuing his monthly, *Ha-Shahar*, from Vienna in 1869. He believed Jews had a national identity that transcended their religion. He used the Hebrew language to strengthen Jewish nationalism among his people. Samuel Leib Citron, who knew Smolenskin, said "there was not one yeshiva in all the Russian Pale to which Smolenskin's *Ha-Shahar* had not found its way. The young people devised cunning ways to deceive their guardians. They read *Ha-Shahar* on the Gemara and under the

Gemara and sat up nights with it . . . The Orthodoxy considered *Ha-Shahar* as unclean, feeding on poison emanating from the anti-divine, while the young people looked upon it with piety and love, as something sacred . . . [It] revolutionized their minds, undermined old ideas infested with traditional moldiness, stimulated them to new ideas. It brought light into the most dismal Jewish byways, rescuing thousands of talented young people who otherwise would have exhausted their talents in sterile pastimes."

But as the nineteenth century wore on, a reaction to the Haskala set in among the writers themselves. We saw it in Peretz. Smolenskin was another to confess its failures. The wave of assimilation had swept many young people away from Jewish identity. Anti-Semitism was on the rise, and pogroms broke out in several parts of Russia. If the slavish imitation of Western ways continued, Smolenskin said, it would end in national suicide. Jewish survival depended upon the recognition of the Jewish people, not only as a religious community, but as a national entity. Jewish history proved, he said, that the religious idea and the national concept were one and inseparable. His modern novel, *The Wanderer in Life's Way*, took his hero through the stages he himself had undergone, and climaxed with the hero dying in defense of Jews during the Odessa pogrom of 1871.

Early in the 1860's a Jewish press emerged, chiefly in Vilna and Odessa. Some of the papers appeared in Hebrew, some in Yiddish. They advocated Haskala, fought against anti-Semitism and for equal rights for Jews, and tried to modernize the Jewish way of life.

Russian censorship crippled their efforts, and few lasted long. By 1871 all were silent, except for Smolenskin's monthly, which reached Russian Jews from Vienna.

As Jewish nationalism mounted, Hebrew as a spoken tongue revived. It had been confined chiefly to the book, but now, powered by the new written literature, it became the core of the Hebrew renaissance. On the tongue and in print it became the vernacular, with dusty clichés cleared out and nineteenth-century modernity introduced.

Swiftly, within two generations, it was renewed as a living language developing with and from Jewish life. Later, with the rebirth of Israel, it would become the language spoken by all the people, used in every aspect of daily life, in schooling and in business, in science and in politics, in war and in peace. Hebrew became a language with a rich secular literature, a literature that could produce a Nobel laureate.

The pioneer of spoken Hebrew was Eliezer Ben Yehuda (1858–1922). He gave all his energy to its revival, using his skills as philologist and editor to adjust Hebrew to the needs of everyday life. His *Dictionary of Ancient and Modern Hebrew* is the indispensable classic in this field.

It was in poetry that the new Hebrew spirit found its greatest expression. The most important pioneering work was done by two poets who broke free of outworn Hebrew rhetoric and created an idiom that came more simply and naturally to a modern Jew's tongue. Chaim Nachman Bialik (1873–1934) was the new poetry's most powerful voice. Born in the Ukraine, he became

Chaim Nachman Bialik, spokesman for the aspirations of the Jewish people. He wrote both in Hebrew and in Yiddish

*YIVO Institute for Jewish Research*

the channel for the aspirations of the Jewish masses. He wrote in both Hebrew and Yiddish, taking from the traditional Jewish culture his diction and symbols. He made available to modern Jews the riches of all the older sources, from Bible and Talmud through the rabbinic literature and the secular Jewish poetry of Arabic Spain. With his strong historical sense, he brought out their timeless and universal humanism.

Bialik's contemporary, Saul Tchernichovsky (1875–1943), born in the Crimea, wrote lyric and epic poetry in Hebrew. He portrayed the martyrdom of both medieval and modern Jewry. He found the bond of common humanity in the widest range of characters. He sought the regeneration of the Jewish people in labor, in cultivation of the sense of beauty, and in the rebellious and heroic spirit of ancient Israel. His work in translation was of equal value, bringing into Hebrew the poems and plays of Homer, Sophocles, Shakespeare, Goethe. For their seminal influence on Hebrew poetry, Bialik and Tchernichovsky have been compared with William Carlos Williams and Ezra Pound.

A little younger was the poet from White Russia, Zalman Schneour (1886–1959). He defied the old conventions in vigorous modern Hebrew, and resurrected the sensual life in verse and fiction. The social upheavals of his time were at the heart of his work. He exalted resistance to injustice and hymned the historical struggle of exiled Israel to retain its identity among the nations.

But it was through Yiddish, the language of the shtetl, that writers reached their greatest audience. In poems, novels, plays, short stories, they mirrored the lives of the

shtetl Jews, sparked a revolt against inertia and dog-
matism, and drew readers on to new horizons. The
Yiddish literature grew in soil fertilized by deep social
change, for by the 1880's the Jewish masses had begun to
awaken, to take their fate in their own hands. They
moved into cities and entered the working class as industrial capitalism took hold in Russia. They organized
trade unions, went on strike, reached out for education
and culture.

Among the early writers to meet their needs were
Isaac Meir Dick (1814–93) and Eliakum Zunser (1836–
1913). Dick's realistic stories and romantic novels were
best-sellers, popular especially with women who bought
his penny booklets at the market or from wandering
peddlers. His critical picture of traditional Jewish life
was enjoyed particularly for the folk humor embedded in
it. Zunser, like Dick born in Vilna, was known as
Eliakum the Bard. His poems, satires, and essays recorded the responses of the Jews in the Pale to life under
the czars. Zunser's work too was circulated in penny
paperbacks and his poems were recited, sung, or chanted
in the home. Like Dick, his goal was to teach ethical
conduct and to plant new ideas in his readers' minds.

In 1875 a humorous Jewish weekly appeared. Called
*Yisrolik*, it was edited by Isaac Joel Linetsky (1839–
1916) and Abraham Goldfaden (1840–1908). Linetsky
had written a novel attacking Hasidic practices, and
Goldfaden was known for a collection of Yiddish songs.
Soon Goldfaden reached new audiences with his plays
and musical comedies, establishing the first modern professional Yiddish theater.

In the last quarter of the nineteenth century three writers appeared whose work earned Yiddish literature worldwide recognition. They were Sholem Jacob Abramowitz (1836–1917), known by his pen name, Mendele Mocher Sforim; Sholem Rabinowitz (1859–1916), who wrote as Sholem Aleichem; and Isaac Leib Peretz (1852–1915). Each wrote in Hebrew too, but it is for their Yiddish creations that they are supremely valued.

The oldest of the group, Mendele, was born in Kapulye in the Lithuanian Pale. He passed an examination for teachers in government-sponsored schools and got a job in a Jewish school in Kamenets. In 1858 he moved to Berdichev, where marriage brought him a wealthy father-in-law who supported him while he wrote. In 1864 his first Yiddish story was serialized. When his father-in-law lost his money, Mendele, now with a family of seven, could barely pay his rent on his earnings from his books. Baron Horace Günzburg became his patron for a few years, until Mendele was hired as principal of a Jewish school in Odessa. The job supported him for the rest of his life.

Mendele stripped the folk language of its heavy Hebrew idioms and shaped it into a flexible instrument for his stories on the Jews penned up in the Pale. His first literary experiments were all in Hebrew, but one day he asked himself:

> What good does the writer's work and thought serve him, if they are of no use to his people? For whom was I working? The question gave me no peace

Mendele Mocher Sforim, the grandfather of Yiddish literature
*YIVO Institute for Jewish Research*

*but placed me in a dilemma. Yiddish, in my time, was an empty vessel, filled only with ridicule, nonsense, and the twaddle of fools who could not speak like human beings . . . People were ashamed to read Yiddish, not wanting to show their backwardness . . . The Hebrew writers, concerned only with the style of sacred language, uninterested in the people, despised Yiddish and mocked it . . . My concern for Yiddish conquered my vanity and I decided, come what may, I would have pity for Yiddish, that rejected daughter, for it was time to do something for our people. . .*

When he wrote his first Yiddish story—it was in 1863—Mendele adopted the pseudonym that means Mendele the Bookseller. His work, as one critic said, "has a kind of dual feeling: every line echoes with disdain for the Jewish life that is past and every chapter ends on a note of sadness that cries out with compassion." In his stories he kept telling people to live better.

*The life of the Jews, although it seems outwardly ugly and dark in color, is inwardly beautiful; a mighty spirit animates it, the divine breath which flutters through it from time to time . . . Israel is the Diogenes of the nations; while his head towers in the heavens and he is occupied with deep meditation concerning God and His wonders, he himself lives in a barrel.*

Critical though Mendele was of Jewish life in the Pale, he loved and identified with the tragicomic characters who crowded his bitter novels. Total commitment as a Jew did not require him to romanticize the Jewish world he sprang from. Half a century of creative work earned him the title of the grandfather of modern Yiddish literature.

Sholem Aleichem was one of Mendele's great literary offspring. (This pen name means "Peace be unto you" in Hebrew, and is a traditional greeting among Jews.) Born in Voronov in the Ukraine, at seventeen he became a teacher of Russian, and at twenty-one a government rabbi. He married a landowner's daughter and went into business to make a living until he quit in 1903 to give all his time to writing. He published his first Yiddish story at the age of twenty-four. It was the first droplet in a powerful flood that would fill twenty-eight volumes of his collected works.

In his own lifetime Sholem Aleichem became the kind of public literary figure that Dickens and Mark Twain were. Like them, he was both a popular entertainer and a major artist. But unlike them he came from a much more homogeneous culture. He could speak for his shtetl society and be recognized as their one true voice, the voice of the Jewish people as a whole. As Irving Howe and Eliezer Greenberg put it:

*Sholem Aleichem gave to the Jews what they instinctively felt was the right and true judgement of their experience: a judgement of love through the medium of irony. Sholem Aleichem is the great poet of Jewish humanism and of Jewish transcendence over the pomp of the world. For the Jews of Eastern*

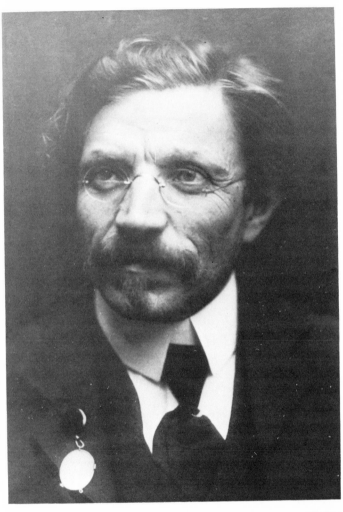

Sholem Aleichem, one of the most popular of modern Yiddish
writers                                    *YIVO Institute for Jewish Research*

*Europe he was protector and advocate; he celebrated
their communal tradition; he defended their style of
life and constantly underlined their passionate urge to
dignity. But he was their judge as well; he ridiculed
their pretensions, he mocked their vanity and he constantly reiterated the central dilemma, that simultane-
ous tragedy and joke, of their existence—the irony of
their claim to being a Chosen People, indeed, the
irony of their existence at all.*

Sholem Aleichem's world is peopled with the ordinary
Jews of the shtetl, but the three most representative ones
are Tevye the Dairyman, the philosopher of the heart;
Menachem Mendel, the luftmensch; and Mottel, the
cantor's son. Tevye is no *nebbish*: his instincts are
healthy; he knows what is good in this world and what is
bad. His defeats do not destroy him. Unable to reshape
the world, he uses humor to sweeten it. In Sholem
Aleichem's stories about children, he introduced something new into Yiddish literature. He portrayed young
boys who resisted being pushed so soon into their
father's world of study and prayer, with its crowded,
dismal atmosphere, its burdens of Torah and mitzvas, its
eternal worry about making a living. The humorist
showed deep insight into childlike feeling. He shared
with the child the gift of carefree laughter.

Sholem Aleichem's stories poured out of him inex-
haustibly. What kind of Yiddish style did he use? Not,
says Maurice Samuel, what we would call a writer's.

*He was a speaker. He chatted about his world. Or*

*put it this way: he let his world flow through him, as though through a funnel. He uses ordinary language; his stories, people, and townlets have the quality of anonymity; they are not thought up; they happen to be there, and Sholem Aleichem calls our attention to them, casually. It is all one long monologue, the recital of a pilgrimage. Certainly it is all transfigured by the passage through his mind, but it is not distorted. The bad is there with the good, the hateful with the heartening . . .*

When Maurice Samuel was a young man, he met Sholem Aleichem on the porch of a New Jersey beach hotel. It was shortly before the writer's death, and Samuel never forgot the encounter.

*I, a youngster of twenty, sat and stared at him, who was already a living legend among his people. A slightly gnomelike elderly little man, with a clever, wrinkled face, kindly, satirical eyes, and a gentle voice, full of tenderness and slyness. Even in repose his face suggested irrepressible amusement, as though invisibly on the tip of his nose a joke were ever balanced neatly on its center of levity. You would have taken him for a Hebrew-teacher, a small town rabbi, perhaps even for a wise old shopkeeper given to books and close observation of his customers; certainly an attractive, even a fascinating personality, full of years and suffering and accumulated comment on life, but not, in heaven's name, a literary genius.*

Peretz was born at a time when the Hasidic tradition was under attack from the new trend of secular thought that was gaining ground among Eastern European Jews. He began to write in Yiddish while still an adolescent, but his first work to be published was a book of poems in Hebrew. For the next ten years he did little writing while practicing law. Then the government disbarred him when a competitor denounced him as a socialist. Needing money, he turned again to writing, this time in Yiddish. "In that language," he said, "are hidden the weeping of our parents, the outcries of many generations, the poison and the bitterness of history. It contains the dearest diamonds—Jewish tears which become hardened before they had dried." Diamonds, but his writing never made him any money to speak of.

In 1890, financed by a rich Warsaw Jew, Peretz toured many shtetls in the Pale to gather economic and cultural data for a report on the life of Polish Jews. Returned from his investigation, he was hired as bookkeeper by the Jewish Civic Center of Warsaw, a job he held until his death. He did all he could to strengthen the Jewish community. The city's Jewish literary life centered on his home.

As an intellectual, Peretz did not reach the mass audiences of the more popular Mendele and Sholem Aleichem. He linked the folk voice of the past with the Jewish renaissance, using a pithy, idiomatic Yiddish. He fought against assimilation and for a dynamic Judaism. His earlier writing is electric with city rhythms and social revolt. Later he reshaped Hasidic tales into parables that

Isaac Leib Peretz. He began to write in Polish, turned to Hebrew, then to Yiddish    *YIVO Institute for Jewish Research*

reflect the dilemmas of the modern intellectual. His influence upon Yiddish writers has been compared with that of Pushkin upon Russian and Emerson upon American culture.

A glimpse of Peretz at home in Warsaw has been left us by Jehiel Isaiah Trunk. The young writer, newspaper-wrapped story in hand, heart pounding, rang the famous man's doorbell. When it opened,

> There stood before us a short, stout figure, with graying short-cropped hair. A long yellow mustache concealed his mouth; the ends of the mustache drooped over the corners of his lips and trembled upon his cheeks. He wore a silk smoking jacket. His shirt collar was open and revealed a short, rather heavy neck. He wore pince-nez, with half lenses. He raised his limpid eyes to us and asked what we wanted.

They spoke in Yiddish, Trunk explaining that he had brought a story for Peretz to read. Then the young man looked around the second-floor apartment.

> Peretz's home overwhelmed me, everything seemed to me full of poetry and fame. His study was a large light room, though the old fashioned windows, set with small panes of glass, seemed somewhat countrified. In the center of the room stood large wooden bowls of full-grown oleander plants, which filled the room with flaming crimson, a crimson that seemed dewy in the light of the sun pouring in. The windows of the study showed a generous portion of sky because there was no building opposite, only the tall factory chimney just opposite the window at which Peretz's desk stood. The desk itself was covered with large vases of flowers that overshadowed everything else, making it seem like a fragrant flowerbed. The walls

*were densely hung with drawings and photographs,
including portraits of Peretz in various poses . . .*

After Peretz read the young writer's story, he said,

*"You have interesting ideas . . . but you don't
know Hebrew. You think in Yiddish and translate
yourself into Hebrew. No, this has no point, why don't
you write Yiddish? Doesn't it suit you, a son-in-law
of the Priveses, to write in the language of the common
herd?"*

Trunk promised to bring him something in Yiddish,
and then Peretz said he'd like to read him something
he'd written that day. Trunk recalled the effect it made
on him.

*It was a prose poem, "Cain and Abel." I would not
today rank it among Peretz's best work. But at that
moment I considered it the greatest spiritual experience of my life. Peretz's voice was unlike any I had
ever heard, at once crusty and tender, metallic as gold
and sweet as the subtlest honey. In this voice Peretz
could express with mastery his emotions and turbu-
lence, his longings and his unquieted temperament.
He could threaten like an enraged lion and be gentle
as the most peaceful dove . . .*

Peretz gave guidance to many such young writers. "To
be Jewish," he said, "is our only way to be human . . .

To find the essence of Jewishness in all places, all times, in all parts of the scattered and dispersed world-folk; to find the soul of all this and to see it lit with the prophetic dream of a human future—that is the task of the Jewish artist."

# 13 WHAT IS TO BE DONE?

O N A SPRING DAY IN 1866, ALEXANDER II was returning from a walk in the Summer Garden in St. Petersburg. A young student standing nearby took out a revolver and pointed it at the czar. As he pulled the trigger, someone shoved his arm aside. The bullet missed its target. The student, Dmitri Karakozov, was immediately seized and turned over to the police.

Karakozov, the son of an impoverished noble family, had been expelled from two universities. He was a member of "Hell," a terrorist cell in a student revolutionary organization. Disgusted with endless radical talk, he wanted action. The Russian masses seemed deaf to propaganda; they needed to be roused from their torpor by an act of revolutionary violence, he decided. When his group refused to join him, he set out to assassinate the czar by himself.

Karakozov missed, but his shot reverberated throughout the empire. Russians crowded churches to give thanks for the czar's deliverance. In theaters, audiences interrupted the performance to demand everyone sing "God Save the Czar." Messages of joy at the czar's escape poured in from the local assemblies and from governments abroad. The public contributed funds to erect a chapel on the sacred spot where the czar had stood when fired at. Over the entrance was placed the message TOUCH NOT MINE ANOINTED.

The gallows quickly put an end to Karakozov's young life. His act gave government reactionaries the chance to pull the brake on the reforms initiated by Alexander II. The abolition of serfdom, the introduction of local government councils, and a new court system were more than enough, they insisted. They seized upon the attempted assassination as proof of what they had argued all along: reform had gone too far and anarchy now threatened the regime. To stop it dead, the czar must expand the police, clamp censorship tighter, revise the educational system, and intensify Russification.

Tired of trouble, and longing for protection, Alexander II gave full rein to reaction. He set up a commission to investigate the assassination attempt. It failed to find any widespread revolutionary organization. But a handful of terrorists was enough for the investigators. They concluded the universities were producing students with no respect for law and order and that the people themselves were fed up with the decline in authority.

In May 1866 the czar proclaimed his new course. His policy would safeguard religion, property rights, and public order. "Orthodoxy, autocracy, and nationality"—they were more solidly enthroned than ever. Any talk of a constitution for Russia or of political freedoms was now a crime against the state.

The key members of Karakozov's revolutionary group were caught and sentenced to hard labor and imprisonment in Siberia. Several leftist publications were closed down. Hundreds of other radicals were rounded up and often sent into exile without trial. Political prisoners were treated so harshly that dozens died, committed suicide, or went insane in prison. Often when suspected revolutionists were acquitted by the courts, police re-arrested them and forced them into exile. Certain acts against the state, especially terrorism against officials, were placed under military courts, which could impose the death penalty.

Karakozov was one of those angry young men who despaired of any basic change in Russian life. The number of radical intellectuals had grown in the late 1850's and early 1860's as Alexander's relaxation of controls allowed some freedom to discuss social and economic questions. But the radicals thought the czar's reforms trivial, promising no real improvement for the empire's suffering millions.

One of the powerful influences on youth's emotion and thought was a novel called *What Is to Be Done?* Published by Chernishevsky in 1864, it became the bible of the radicals. It held out the vision of a socialist society and advocated workers' cooperatives and women's liberation. Its heroine, Vera Pavlovna, wants independence and equality in her sexual life, and at the same time a career. She sets up cooperatives of seamstresses that divide profits equally among the workers and also educate them. The leading male character, Rakhmetev, trains himself like a Spartan in selfless devotion to his future revolutionary mission.

The official view of such young radicals is reflected in the records of the political police. They describe Vera as a woman "with hair cut short, wearing blue glasses, slovenly dressed, loath to use comb and soap, and living in common law matrimony with one or more members of the male sex, who are equally repelling."

The radicals were encouraged at first by the distrust the peasants showed for the czar's emancipation program. The former serfs struggled against the restrictions and obligations still imposed upon them, and even used armed force against authority. In Kazan province in 1861 they refused to obey the officials. Troops came in and killed or wounded 350 peasants. The rural unrest encouraged the radicals to demonstrate, and many more students turned to socialist thinkers as their guide. Manifestos poured off underground presses, addressed to peasants, soldiers, and students, calling for open revolutionary activity in response to the government's repressive measures. What the people needed, one said, was "land and freedom." When St. Petersburg University was shut down because the government thought it a hotbed of revolution, Herzen's journal, *The Bell*, urged the expelled students "to go to the people." That phrase became one of the most famous slogans of the Russian revolutionary movement. Another manifesto called "Young Russia" urged youth to place itself at the head of the masses and lead them to a revolution, a revolution that would wipe out the institutions of state, family, and church, and under a dictatorship build a new Russian society based on socialism and the peasant commune.

Turgenev's novel of 1862, *Fathers and Sons*, creates in the character of Bazarov a young radical taken as typical of his generation. Opposite such a youth the novelist poses his weak and ineffectual elders, members of the gentry class to which Turgenev himself belonged. The critic Pisarev considers Bazarov a positive hero because as a nihilist he negates the traditions and values of the older generation. His example, Pisarev writes, would help free the sons from the superstition and ignorance that crippled their fathers.

That same year the first revolutionary organization was founded, taking the name of "Land and Freedom." It survived scarcely twelve months, but it set the example for a movement that would prepare the people for revolution.

The conflict between fathers and sons had broken out in Jewish life before Turgenev wrote his famous novel. When a young man or woman in the shtetl chose to abandon Orthodoxy, it meant a break with family and home. They usually went one of two ways. Some gave up their Jewish identity to merge with the revolutionary movement. They saw that the czar's minor reforms had not solved the Jewish question. Only a tiny part of the Jewish population had seen its lot eased. And as reaction intensified control, the dream of Jewish emancipation faded. Only a revolution gave hope for liberation. The young Jewish radicals were captivated by the call to "go to the land"; the revolt would begin through work with the peasant.

Others left Judaism to become part of the secular Yiddish world, joining one of the political or cultural movements within it. Some who repudiated their Jewishness later came back to it, after discovering that Russian revolutionaries too could be anti-Semitic, that socialism would not necessarily give the Jews full equality and liberate them from persecution.

It was part of the tragic war between the generations, one side totally committed to Orthodoxy, the other side blind to historical Judaism, national as well as religious.

At the end of the 1860's, the government sent to officials throughout the empire a manual on how to cope with the "internal enemy"—the Jews. It was based upon the writings of Joel Branfman, a Jew from Minsk who converted to Christianity and turned spy and informer for the government. In essence, the manual insisted the government must destroy the Jewish community and all its institutions or Russia would be taken over by the Jews' worldwide "secret government."

Soon after, a pogrom against the Jews broke out in Odessa. Greeks and Jews alike had built Odessa into a prosperous city. But the two groups were strong commercial rivals. The Greeks decided to scare their competitors out through a pogrom. They excited the Russian populace with a rumor that the Jews had desecrated a church. The pogrom began on Easter Sunday, 1871. Mobs of Greeks and Russians ran wild in the streets for three straight days, beating up Jews and smashing and looting hundreds of their homes and shops. It ended on the fourth day when the government finally intervened. An "investigation" concluded that the violence against the Jews was only a "crude protest" of the masses against the "exploiters."

About the same time, one of the czar's numerous commissions on the Jews decided that whatever remained of Jewish self-government must be eradicated. Schools, mutual-aid societies, community organizations —all must go. But the Pale of Settlement had to be continued. A commission spokesman warned how dangerous it would be to let the Jews outside the Pale because "the plague that now affects only the western provinces will engulf the entire empire." This concern for quarantining the Jewish "plague" had proved for years to be quite elastic. The historian Simon Dubnow points this out in relation to the Jews and agriculture.

*During the reign of Alexander I and Nicholas I colonization was encouraged in the barren southern steppes. But under Alexander II, when Novorussia was no longer in need of artificial colonization, and the farmland was needed for its "own" peasants, the government ceased to encourage Jewish colonization. Shortly after, the Jews were deprived of the largest tracts of land, which were in turn distributed among Russian peasants.*

Anti-Semitism was forming into an explicit movement and shifting from the religious to the political sphere. Conservative forces in Russia, like those in Germany and France in the same period, pumped up the Jewish issue. They exploited anti-Semitism as one day Hitler would, if far more skillfully. The folklore of anti-Semitism deposited in the minds of the peasants over the centuries was brought to the surface by vicious men whose aim was to turn the poison to political account.

The revolutionary rumblings in Russia exposed dissatisfaction with the way things were. Instead of honestly facing its internal problems, the government used diversionary tactics. On the powerless minority of Jews was laid the responsibility for the evils the people were suffering from.

In high governmental and social circles anti-Semitism became more and more blatant. Edicts and exclusions continued. A military-service law added new discriminatory measures against the Jews in the 1870's. In the Russo-Turkish War of 1877–8, many Jews died to emancipate their "brother Slavs." The government gave no praise to their sacrifice; instead, from all the military provisioners who were abusing their contracts, it singled out a Jewish firm for public attack. At the Congress of Berlin in 1878, the participating nations favored granting the Jews of Rumania, Serbia, and Bulgaria equal rights. But the Russian delegate fought against it.

A Catholic priest defrocked for "unheard-of crimes and a corrupt life" published a book *On the Use of Christian Blood by Jews.* The government bought copies to distribute among the Russian police. In 1878, another ritual murder trial was staged, against nine Jews in the Caucasus. They were exonerated, but the popular superstition about ritual murder was once again spread on the pages of the Russian press.

The Jewish question in Russia was not isolated from other problems, of course. As Henrik Sliosberg, one of the Jewish lawyers who fought hardest against czarist anti-Semitic persecution, pointed out:

*Jews were not the only ones denied civic rights;*

*actually 90 percent of native Russian peasants were*
*without rights. There was high-handedness not just*
*toward Jews alone, but toward other nationals as well;*
*the Jews, however, received the hardest blows from*
*Russian reaction, and the persecution of Jews became*
*the barometer of the political outlook at any given*
*time.*

Renewed oppression by the czar drove still more
young Jews into the revolutionary movement. Many
joined the Populists, a socialist group that saw the peasant commune as central to the ideal society they wanted
to build. Students from the universities, the technical
schools, and the high schools made up the bulk of the
Populists. Many were from the upper classes and the
clergy, with a proportionately large number of Jews
among them. These sons and daughters were the first
generation raised on secular lines, knowing little of
Jewish tradition. Some were hostile to everything Jewish.
They feared their Jewishness would block them from
"going to the people." They often came from families
which had assimilated. Fighting for a revolutionary new
society meant entering a world in which all religions
would disappear. There would be no Jews, no distinction
between themselves and everyone else.

That they felt so inferior is due in part to the Russian
literature they were raised on. Pushkin, Gogol, Lermon-
tov, Dostoevsky, Turgenev could not depict Jews as
anything but vile creatures. Russian fiction, drama, and
poetry portrayed the Jew as dirty, dishonest, contempt-
ible; as parasite, opportunist, fiend. The Jew would do

anything for money, betray anyone for his own advantage. He deserved only the worst treatment. Sensitive as they might be to all other human souls, when it came to the Jew, the Russian writers saw him as subhuman. Nor did the socialist theoreticians to whom the young radicals looked for guidance offer any opposing view. Neither Marx nor Bakunin had a good word to say for the Jew, rich or poor. Rather, their "scientific" opinions only strengthened the self-hatred of young Jewish revolutionaries.

In the beginning, the Populists believed the overthrow of czarism would be a simple thing to do, perhaps even bloodless. They had only to bring light to the "dark people." Once shown their true interests, the peasants would make the revolution.

The young Jewish radicals were fascinated by this messianic vision of a kingdom of heaven on earth. Moritz Winchevsky, recalling his feelings then, said, "We were all Narodniki and the peasants were our brothers." But the peasants—four fifths of the population—were largely illiterate, while most of the Jews, no matter how badly off, could at least read and write and be reached through the printed word in Yiddish. One of the Jewish Populists, Aaron Liberman, tried to convert the Jewish masses to socialism with a Hebrew monthly. The government banned it in Russia and it soon went bankrupt.

Since the peasants could not read the revolutionary word, the radicals had to make them hear it. Following Herzen's "To the People!" about two thousand Populist students took to the countryside in what became known as the "mad summer" of 1874. They penetrated deep into Russia, expecting to find peasants waiting for the word to rise up against the czar and seize the land.

But the ex-serfs, though they lived in terrible poverty, were bound by deep religious faith and an almost instinctive loyalty to the czar. Not the czar but landlords and officials were their enemies, as they saw it. When the call for revolutionary action came, they did not respond. Instead, they led some of the radicals, especially those already anti-intellectual, toward a mystical belief that in the rural folk there resided an innate wisdom from which the Populists could learn.

Most of the young radicals, their naïve faith shaken, soon became disillusioned. But the Populist movement was not destroyed. It changed, finding other approaches to revolution. By 1878 a new secret society was active, reviving the name "Land and Freedom." It set up a tighter organization and stricter discipline. An attempt at a political demonstration in St. Petersburg was swiftly crushed by the police. The leaders were arrested and thrown into the Peter-Paul fortress. Such old ways of working, it was apparent, were no longer effective.

The new way was to be terrorism. Basically, a policy of frustration. The masses had shown themselves indifferent to making a revolution. If they would not help themselves, the enlightened few must do it for them. But how? Through the direct method of terror. Assassinate the most unpopular leaders of the government, the reasoning went, and the regime would collapse, giving way to the new order.

It was not a fresh idea. Terror had been tried sporadically in Russia for the past quarter of a century. But these young revolutionaries meant to do it differently, in a systematic and sustained way.

It began early in 1878. The first target was the St. Petersburg police chief, General Fedor Trepov, who had ordered flogging of an imprisoned revolutionary for not taking off his cap when the chief passed. In January Vera Zasulich shot Trepov, but lacked the skill to more than wound him. To the government's consternation, a jury acquitted her because of Trepov's reputation for cruelty and she disappeared underground.

Educated Russians openly showed their sympathy for Zasulich. In the next few months there were serious strikes in St. Petersburg. Zasulich's act was followed by more attempts on the lives of officials, with the terrorists resisting arrest and sometimes shooting it out with the police who raided their hideouts. That summer the chief of the czar's Third Section of gendarmes was himself assassinated. Now government and public alike were convinced an army of terrorists was operating. In actuality, their total number, scattered in small groups, was probably no more than a thousand. Ignorance and fear led the government to launch a massive campaign against sedition and terrorism. Officials were given the power to expel undesirables, exile the dangerous, shut down periodicals, and try in military courts any civilians suspected of acts of terrorism. Relentlessly the czar's men raided, arrested, expelled, jailed, executed. They could not help but be indiscriminate under such orders, and the innocent were caught as often as the guilty were missed.

The sweeping attack only heightened the terror. In 1879 Prince Dmitri Kropotkin was killed. His assassin was Gregory Goldenberg, a young Jew. When Goldenberg was arrested many months later, he was tricked into talking to an informer-cellmate, and gave away names, methods, and other details of his terrorist group. When he realized what he had done, he hanged himself in his cell.

The mounting use of terror caused a split in the Land and Freedom society. One group, calling themselves the Black Partition, determined to go on with propaganda work in the villages. They put their trust in reason and persuasion. The revolution would be justified only if it were the work of the people for whose benefit it was supposed to take place. The others, impatient at the slow work of education and frustrated by the Russian conditions which defeated most attempts at reform, formed the People's Will. It was a tiny, highly disciplined group of professional revolutionaries ready to justify any means by the one end—revolution.

The two groups divided funds and materials amicably and went their separate ways. The refusal of the Black Partition to adopt conspiratorial methods made it easy for spies to penetrate their group. The police smashed their printing press early in 1880 and the leaders fled abroad.

The wave of terror and the dissatisfaction with the government's conduct of the war with Turkey produced a political crisis for the czar. The educated classes wanted to return to the reforms of the 1860's and even asked for constitutional government. The ruling circle was shaky, uncertain, divided over how best to meet the serious challenge. If the revolutionary danger was as great as it seemed, would it be better to make concessions to the people? Or better to crush the opposition with even more violence?

# 14 1881—THE TERRIBLE YEAR

I N AUGUST 1879 TERRORISTS OF THE
People's Will sentenced Alexander II to death. For
nearly two years they carried on a desperate campaign
with but a single objective—to kill the czar. They made
no preparations for the seizure of power. They gave no
thought to what might happen upon the czar's death.
Their only hope was that the people would rise up and
take their fate into their own hands.

Three times they planted dynamite to blow up the
imperial train. Each time something went wrong. Then
they turned to another scheme. They placed dynamite
under the floor of the czar's dining room in the Winter
Palace. The charge was set to go off just as a state dinner
was about to begin. The explosion occurred on time, but
the czar's entry had been delayed. The victims were
eleven guardsmen killed and fifty-six others wounded as
the walls and floors caved in.

Government morale was shattered, the citizens in
panic, many fleeing the city. St. Petersburg was put
under a state of siege, with armed guards patrolling the
streets, curfew imposed, and the royal family in hiding.

The czar appointed a commission with dictatorial

powers to root out sedition and made General Mikhail Loris-Melikov its head. A few days later, a terrorist tried—but failed—to kill the general. The young man was arrested and hanged within forty-eight hours.

Loris-Melikov pressed the czar to make reforms in domestic policy. The terror, he argued, was the diseased outgrowth of deep dissatisfaction among the people. Peasants, students, the clergy, local officials—all were embittered because they felt the government did not listen to their needs. The czar, he said, should get rid of tyrannical and corrupt officials, relax the censorship, and revive the spirit of the early years of his reign. Alexander was impressed. He moved to liberalize the government. Meanwhile, police informers and agents provocateurs helped hunt down scores of terrorists. Twenty-one were executed. It was the price they paid for six unsuccessful attempts on the czar's life in a span of eight months.

The reforms made by the czar were superficial. He abolished the Third Section but transferred its gendarmes to the state police and continued their old functions. As terrorist activity diminished, the mood of crisis passed. The czar listened agreeably to a scheme for expanding his State Council so as to give his rule the appearance of broader popular participation.

As his advisers drafted a manifesto announcing the changes, the terrorists were completing plans for another assault upon Alexander. Director of the operation was Andrey Zhelyabov, the son of serfs. Early in 1881 he and Sophie Perovskaya, a daughter of aristocrats, took an apartment in St. Petersburg for the plotters to work from. They watched closely the czar's movements about the capital: he followed a fixed routine on Sundays. Now they could design his death.

They rented a cheese shop and at night mined their way beneath it to a point under the street the czar's carriage nearly always passed over. They chose Sunday, March 1, for the day of execution. If his carriage took the usual route, he would be blown to pieces by the underground cylinders of dynamite. If that failed, bomb throwers stationed in several places would have their turn.

Meanwhile, the police started to grope their way toward the heart of the People's Will. Zhelyabov was picked up on suspicion. But the terrorists had allowed for that possibility; they could go on without him. Suspicious neighbors told the police something strange was going on at the cheese shop, and on February 28 they raided it. They failed to detect the concealed entrance to the tunnel where the dynamite was buried, or even to notice the earth piled under a bed. They left after chatting idly about the terrorists' cat.

The next morning was March 1. With two bombs in her lap, Sophie Perovskaya drove to her rendezvous with six other terrorists, who were armed with two more bombs. Some would be lookouts, the others throwers. They went over their signals and procedure one last time, then moved to their stations.

It was about two o'clock now, and the sky was clouded over. The wind whistled over the snowy streets, crowded with worshippers on their way home from church. The Emperor's carriage raced back to the Winter Palace by way of the Ekaterinsky Canal. Cossack guards rode beside it and ahead, while behind were two sleighs filled with policemen. When the czar's carriage came abreast of the first terrorist—Rysakov, a nineteen-year-old factory worker—he threw his bomb under it. Flames shot up, and as the sound of the explosion smashed the Sunday quiet, the back of the carriage tore apart. The frightened horses bolted ahead, dragging the royal carriage a hundred yards more before the coachman could rein them to a halt. The police rushed up and opened the door, expecting to find death. But the czar stepped out, pale, shaken, and limping slightly. The police urged him to return at once to the Winter Palace, but he wanted to go back to where the bomb had been hurled. A crowd had gathered, screaming, shouting, pushing to see the captured terrorist. On the snow lay a wounded Cossack and a dying boy. The czar walked toward them, his officers failing to restrain him. They all moved like sleepwalkers. As the czar edged his way close to the spot where the bomb had exploded, another of the terrorists, a nobleman, Grinevitsky, leaned against a wall, watching him. When the czar was two feet away, Grinevitsky flung a bomb at his feet. Stone, flesh, snow, blood, fire fountained high in the air. The bomb's roar faded, replaced by screaming. Then silence.

The czar's legs had been shattered. Blood gushed from all parts of his body. Around him lay twenty others, dying in the street, Grinevitsky among them.

The czar, still alive, was taken to the palace, where he died an hour later. Grinevitsky died soon after. Rysakov was beaten by the police but refused to give his identity. That night St. Petersburg was full of rumors that the czar had been assassinated at the order of high officials who did not want even the slightest concession made to liberalism. But the next day the People's Will issued a manifesto taking responsibility for the murder.

*Alexander II, the tormentor of the people, has been put to death by us, Socialists. He was killed because he did not care for his people, burdened them with unauthorized taxes, deprived the peasants of their land and surrendered the workers to the mercy of plunderers and exploiters. He did not give the people freedom: he did not listen to their griefs and their tears. He defended only the rich and lived himself in the utmost luxury, while the people went hungry.*

*The Czar's servants, from the village police to the high officials, plundered the people and barbarously maltreated the peasants; and these servants of the Czar were especially protected and rewarded by the Czar. Those who stood out for the people he hanged or exiled to Silbeia.*

*So he was killed. A Czar should be a good shepherd, ready to lay down his life for his flock: Alexander II was a ravening wolf and a terrible death has struck him. Now a new Czar, Alexander III, climbs to the throne. He must not be allowed to behave like his father. May he proceed to hold general elections in the villages and towns and in all the factories. May he recognize the sorrows and deep needs of the people, and go forward into the truth!*

If measured only by the czar's death, the plot of the

People's Will was a success. But from the point of view of those who sought social justice and the progress of liberty, it was an unmitigated disaster. It led only to further repression and reaction.

The public was shocked and numbed by the news. The workers did not rise up in the cities. The peasants thought Alexander had been assassinated by noblemen who wanted serfdom restored. The students did nothing but refuse to contribute to wreaths for the dead emperor.

It was a defeat for the police, but they quickly recovered, and captured the rest of the conspirators. Rysakov broke down, repented his part, and gave information. The others stood by their convictions.

The trial was swift, the verdict guilty, the sentence death by hanging. On April 3, the prisoners were dressed in black, and a placard reading CZARICIDE fastened to their chests. They were taken in tumbrels to Semeonovsky Square, where eighty thousand people were gathered to witness the hangings.

Hardly were the trapdoors sprung when the new emperor, Alexander III, issued a manifesto announcing the end of all reforms. "The voice of God commands us to rule with faith in the power and the truth of the autocratic authority, which we are called upon to confirm and to preserve."

It was the end, too, of the People's Will. Their spirit was exhausted.

In place of a constitution, the new czar imposed what he called "the law of reinforced security." He gave dictatorial power over the citizenry to his governors. It was a Magna Carta for police terror, renewed annually for the next twenty-five years. For his chief adviser the czar selected Konstantin Pobedonostzev, a fanatical reactionary who believed in a police state guided by the church. His slogan was "Russia for Russians."

By Russians, of course, he meant Orthodox Christians; Jews were aliens, and aliens out to rule the world. Under this man and his czar, anti-Semitism was transformed into violence against Jews. The Russian nationalist press had become openly hostile, hinting that the Jews were behind the assassination. Officials left the capital on unexplained missions to the south of Russia, where they discussed with local police chiefs a probable "outburst of the people's indignation against the Jews," implying that it would be better for the police not to thwart the people. A rumor spread of a czarist edict permitting attacks upon Jews during the coming Easter.

In mid-April, pogroms exploded all over southwestern Russia. The first attack upon the Jews was launched at Elizavetgrad on Easter Sunday. A mob ravaged and plundered the large Jewish quarter for two days under the eye of the military. The terror spread in waves as the mobs cried, "Look for the Jew!"

In the next days and weeks the bloody fever raged through 160 cities and villages in the provinces of Kiev and Chernigov and Poltava and Kherson and Ekaterinoslav. Leaders of the mobs were not local people but Russians from the north. Bands of thugs came down by train to spearhead the riots. Investigators were convinced the pogroms were organized and financed by a group of right-wing terrorists known as the "Sacred League."

Among their leaders who held high office was von Drenteln, governor general of Kiev.

As soon as one pogrom was over, the hoodlums shifted to another district to repeat their performance. Their tactics became familiar: first, placards appeared accusing the Jews of being terrorists and the assassins of the czar; then came newspaper stories repeating the charges; and finally the whispered report that the czar himself was allowing "three days to plunder the Jews."

When the mob spirit had been whipped up, a quarrel would be picked with a Jewish shopkeeper, usually a liquor merchant. A fight would break out, the liquor would be raided, and the drunken mob would rampage through the Jewish district. The police and the military, who could have ended the threatening situation with a word, almost never acted. When they did, it was against those Jews who tried to defend themselves.

What happened in the first pogrom, at Elizavetgrad, where fifteen thousand Jews lived, was reported by a government commission. Since it was never intended for publication, it's undoubtedly free of the official lies one would otherwise expect.

*On the night of April 15, an attack was launched on Jewish homes, particularly taverns, in the outskirts of the city, during which one Jew was killed. About seven o'clock in the morning of April 16, the disorders were renewed, spreading through the city with enormous force. Clerks and servants of saloons and hotels, artisans, coachmen, lackeys, officers' attendants, non-*

*combatant soldiers—all these elements joined the movement.*

*The city presented an unusual sight: the streets were covered with feathers and cluttered with broken furniture; doors and windows shattered; an unruly throng rampaging in all directions, yelling and shriek-ing, pursuing its task of destruction unhindered; and as a supplement to this scene—complete indifference on the part of the local non-Jewish residents toward the pogrom in progress.*

*The militia called upon to restore law and order had no definite instructions, and at each new assault of the rabble the armed force had to wait for orders from its own superiors or those of the police. Under such an attitude of the militia, the anarchical mob—smashing houses and shops in full view of the passive garrison—could only conclude that its destructive progress was not illegal, but rather authorized by the government . . . In the evening the disorders intensified, because a mass of peasants had arrived in the city from the neighboring villages in hope of confiscating some Jewish possessions. On April 17 an infantry battalion restored law and order in Elizavetgrad.*

In Kiev the initial stages were the same, except that here the police advised the Jews not to leave their shops or go outdoors on Sunday, April 26. Why, the Jews won-dered, did the police urge them to hide when the city was full of troops who could easily prevent disorder? But Elizavetgrad was a lesson to be heeded, and the Jews stayed off the streets that fateful Sunday. Nevertheless,

While police look on, a Jew is attacked during the pogroms of 1881 in Kiev. That year pogroms broke out in nearly fifty towns of this region  *The Bettmann Archive*

at noon in the Jewish district called Podol, according to an eyewitness account:

> *The air suddenly reverberated with shrieking, whistling and whooping, and roaring laughter. A horde of youths, artisans and laborers was on the march. The destruction of Jewish houses had begun. Windows and doors were flying, and soon all sorts of objects were*

*being hurled from dwellings and shops. The mob then attacked the synagogue and, notwithstanding the sturdy bolts and locks and shutters, it was broken into without much ado. The Scrolls of the Law were torn into scraps, trampled into the muck and destroyed. The Christian population escaped the hoodlums by displaying icons in the windows, and marking crosses on shutters and gates. In the course of the pogrom, troops, Cossacks and infantry patrolled the streets of Podol. The soldiers signalled and occasionally surrounded the rabble, and issued orders for it to disperse, but the latter grew ever more fierce in its assaults.*

At night, the drunken mob attacked in the suburbs and set fire to Jewish homes. They beat some Jews to death and threw others into bonfires. The next day the troops surrounded the mob and fired into it, wounding and killing a few. The pogrom stopped at once. About a thousand Jewish homes and shops had been destroyed, several scores of Jews had been wounded or killed, and a score of women had been raped.

With Kiev setting the example, some fifty villages and towns in the same province followed through with their own pogroms. Except that when a trainload of pogromists reached Berdichev, a Jewish self-defense militia was waiting for them armed with clubs. The "visitors" took one look and decided not to get off the train. Such self-defense was rare then, and made possible only because the police chief had been bribed to permit it.

That same spring, fires swept across the Pale of Settlement, burning down thousands of Jewish homes. The torch was lit chiefly in those places where the authorities had prevented pogroms. The fires, everyone understood, were another way of delivering the same message to the Jews. Minsk was one of the places badly hit. Two thirds of its fifty thousand inhabitants were Jews. The flames destroyed a fifth of the city. In a few hours, one thousand of the wooden houses burned down, and twenty-one of the synagogues. Ten thousand men, women, and children were left homeless.

By early May the pogrom fever seemed to have subsided. The government showed little concern for the victims. It inquired instead whether the pogroms were not part of a larger revolutionary plot, directed in the first stage against the Jews as a merchant class, and to be turned next against the Russian merchants, gentry, and officials. The czar himself said the pogroms were "most likely the doing of anarchists." And added that hatred for the Jews arose from their economic "supremacy" and their "exploiting" of the Russian people. This "exploitation" theory became the official justification for the pogroms and for repressive measures taken against the Jews.

The victims of the pogroms desperately needed help, but the authorities interfered with attempts to collect funds. They went further: they began to expel by the thousands Jews who were said to be living "illegally" in Moscow, Odessa, and other cities. While most pogromists got off with nothing or with light sentences, the courts punished Jews arrested for defending themselves.

The anti-Semites took these acts as encouragement to

pick up the pogroms where they had left off. In late June a second series of outrages began which lasted through the summer. At their height, the semi-official newspaper, *Novoye Vremya*, headlined an article on the violence against the Jews with a parody of Hamlet, "To Beat or Not to Beat?"—and advised its readers it was necessary to beat.

In the fall, there was another lull. But on Christmas Day the blow fell on the Jews of Warsaw. The pogrom gangs went wild in the streets. When the authorities ended it on the third day, forty-five hundred Jewish homes, shops, and synagogues had been devastated and looted. It was the pattern seen everywhere: plunder for two days and stop on the third.

And so the year 1881 ended. It has gone down in the Jewish calendar as one of the terrible years, a year of atrocities, a year of horror, a year when barbarism again besieged Jewry.

It was a year that would radically change the course of Jewish history.

# 15 A PERMANENT
## LEGAL POGROM

THE YEAR 1882 OPENED WITH RUMORS that the czar had still worse things in store for the Jews. It was easy to believe, especially when the Minister of the Interior announced to the press that the government wished to get rid of the Jews. They should use the one right they had, he said—the right to emigrate.

Protest was impossible in a police state. The Jews chose public mourning as the way to demonstrate their feelings. On January 18, fasting and prayer took place in many cities. In St. Petersburg the Jewish community gathered at the great synagogue. They chanted the hymns of martyrdom, and the rabbi spoke, describing in a trembling voice Russia's torture of the Jews. "The congregation gave way to a long, drawn-out wail," said an eyewitness; "everyone wept—the old and the young, the poor in long gaberdines and the elegantly dressed . . . This heartbreaking wailing, this outcry of the collective misfortune, lasted some two or three minutes . . . The rabbi could not continue his address; covering his face with his hands, he wept like a child."

As spring came on, rumors of plans for more pogroms circulated. Balta, a town in Podolia province, was said to be a prime target. The city had three times as many Jews as Christians, and the Jews made secret plans for self-defense. On March 29, during Easter Week, the violence began. The Jews forced the hoodlums to retreat at first, but when police and soldiers appeared, the mob surged back. Instead of dispersing it, the government forces began to beat the Jews with rifle butts and sabers. Then,

> *The houses which were not marked with a cross were invaded by the mob. Doors were beaten in, show-windows demolished, window-frames torn out. Furniture was thrown out of windows, crockery smashed, house-linen torn up, with a joy in destruction both childlike and savage. The mob took untold delight in ripping open featherbeds and down-quilts, and sending the contents drifting in the air like a fall of snow.*
>
> *In several places the pleasure the mob took in sheer destruction overcame their rapacious instincts. Peasants who came from their villages with wagons to take away their share of booty were repeatedly driven away by the rioters. For in certain boroughs, after the house-gear was destroyed, the houses went—floors and roofs being carried away, and nothing left standing but the bare stone walls. Not even the synagogues and cemeteries were spared by popular fury. The tombs were desecrated and the rolls of the Torah defiled.*
>
> *The mob naturally made first for the taverns and taprooms. Barrels were staved in; whiskey ran down the streets; men lay down in the gutters flat on their stomachs, to gorge themselves with the stuff. In sev-*

*eral localities, women, crazed with drink, gave pure spirits to swallow to infants two or three years old, that they might forever remember these glorious days. Others brought their small children to the ruins of Jewish homes, there to bid them "to remember the judgment they had seen overtake the Jews."*

News of that savage scene was censored. Court records revealed later that 1,250 dwellings and shops had been destroyed, and fifteen thousand people had been impoverished through loss of home, property, and merchandise. Forty Jews had been murdered or seriously injured, 170 had been more lightly hurt, and twenty women had been raped. Again, the pogrom halted only on the third day, when the governor came in.

The outbreak of the pogroms was a hard blow to the enlightenment. Many maskilim took it as proof that all attempts to draw closer to the dominant majority were useless. Moses Leib Lilienblum, the influential Hebrew writer who championed the rising secular generation, was thirty-eight in 1881. He wrote:

*During the pogroms, a native woman, ragged and drunk, danced in the streets, joyously shouting: "This is our country, this is our country." Can we say the same, even without dancing in the streets, without being drunk? Yes, we are aliens, not only here but in all Europe, for it is not our fatherland. Now I understand the word "anti-Semitism." This is the secret of our affliction in exile. Even in Alexandria, in the time of the Second Temple, and in all the lands of our*

> *dispersion, we were aliens, unwanted guests . . . Yet*
> *we dream we will become children of the European*
> *nations, children with equal rights. What can be more*
> *fatuous? For we are aliens and will remain aliens . . .*
> *Our future is fearful, without a spark of hope or a ray*
> *of light—slaves, aliens, strangers forever.*

What about the response in the shtetl to pogroms? Like fires and floods, says *Life Is with People*, pogroms are treated as "acts of God," catastrophes that come from outside.

> *There is usually no defense organization. If orga-*
> *nized resistance is attempted by the prosteh or by*
> *young people who have broken away from traditional*
> *attitudes, it is criticized by the very orthodox as "un-*
> *Jewish." One pleads with God for help and mercy.*
> *Perhaps one sends a delegation to the leader of the*
> *attacking group. But to fight back is the exception*
> *rather than the rule.*
>
> *This passivity cannot be attributed simply to fear of*
> *death. There are too many instances of Jews who have*
> *accepted avoidable death rather than violate the Sab-*
> *bath . . .*

That there were attempts at self-defense is evidenced by what happened at Berdichev, and again at Odessa, where students of the local university organized units which managed at times to drive the thugs away from Jewish homes.

And what of liberal Russia? Its voice was silent. There was almost no protest against the pogroms from the great Russian writers. Turgenev and Tolstoy said nothing. Like Dostoevsky, Turgenev was openly anti-Semitic. Perhaps the sole exception was M. E. Saltykov-Shchedrin, who wrote:

> *History has never recorded in its pages a question more difficult, more inhuman, more painful than the Jewish question . . . No history is more heartrending than the history of unending torture by one man of another.*

Liberal Russia, poisoned by anti-Semitism, accepted the line taken by the government: that the pogroms were merely a "people's tribunal" over the Jews. Even worse was the radical response to the pogroms. Some of the radicals adopted the tactic of fusing class with national antagonism. Thus they hoped the violence against the "Jewish exploiters" would be the first step in the awakening of the masses, a step that would be followed by riots against landlords, aristocrats, and government officials.

On August 30, 1881, the executive committee of the People's Freedom group appealed to the Ukrainian people with a leaflet which justified and praised the pogroms.

> *Good people, honest Ukrainian people! Life has become hard in the Ukraine, and it keeps getting harder. The damned police beat you, the landowners devour you, the kikes, the dirty Judases, rob you. People in the Ukraine suffer most of all from the*

*kikes. Who has seized the land, the woodlands, the taverns? The kikes. Whom does the peasant beg with tears in his eyes to let him near his own land? The kikes. Wherever you look, whatever you touch, everywhere the kikes. The kike curses the peasant, cheats him, drinks his blood. The kikes make life unbearable. Workers, arise! Wreak your vengeance on the land-owners; pillage the Jews; kill the officials!*

To the Jewish socialist, Pavel Axelrod, who had fled abroad in 1874 to escape the czarist police, such a leaflet was shocking. He wrote a pamphlet to explain the disillusionment of young Jewish radicals with the revolutionary movement. But his own friends argued it would be a mistake to issue it: it would alienate the Russian masses from the revolution. So Axelrod suppressed his pamphlet.

Chaim Weizmann had something to say about the peculiar attitude of some radicals to Jewishness. It applied then and still applies today.

*They would not tolerate in the Jewish youth any expression of separate attachment to the Jewish people, or even special awareness of the Jewish problem. Yet the Jewish youth was not essentially assimilationist; its bonds with its people were genuine and strong; it was only by doing violence to their inclinations and upbringing that these young men and women had turned their backs, at the bidding of the revolutionary leaders, on the peculiar bitterness of the Jewish lot. My resentment of Lenin and Plekhanov*

*and the arrogant Trotsky was provoked by the con-*
*tempt with which they treated any Jew who was*
*moved by the fate of his people and animated by a*
*love of its history and its tradition. They could not*
*understand why a Russian Jew should want to be any-*
*thing but a Russian. They stamped as unworthy, as*
*intellectually backward, as chauvinistic and immoral,*
*the desire of any Jew to occupy himself with the*
*sufferings and destiny of Jewry.*

News of the Russian pogroms horrified the world
outside. The facts leaked out so slowly that it was
January 1882 before the London *Times* ran a series
called "The Persecution of the Jews in Russia." The
graphic details of the mass violence rallied popular support for diplomatic action in behalf of the Jews and for
material aid to the victims. Meetings, speeches, resolu-
tions urged the British government to act, but its response was so mild the Russians were little concerned.

In several countries relief funds to help the Jews
emigrate from Russia were organized. Victor Hugo
headed the French committee. A huge protest rally was
held in New York as the first refugees from Russia
arrived. The U.S. Congress called on the President to
request the czar to protect his Jewish subjects against
violence.

The Russian Minister of the Interior, Count Ignatiev,
organized regional conferences to look into the causes of
the pogroms. But at the same time he bemoaned "the
tragic situation of the Christian population" in those
very areas where the Jews had been savaged. The aim

was clearly to whitewash the regime. The inquiries provided a forum for anti-Semites to slander the Jews as thieves, swindlers, parasites, and enemies of the state. When Jews tried to refute the charges they were not allowed to speak.

Ignatiev's "investigation" produced what the government wanted: accusations against the Jews and proposals

Chanting the Book of Lamentations in a Polish synagogue. From a painting by Horovitz, 1870

for repressive measures that would strike at the Jews more effectively than the blind rage of mobs.

The outcome was a kind of permanent legal pogrom. The form it took was a series of regulations entitled "Temporary Orders Concerning the Jews." The use of "temporary" was a trick, for the orders stayed in effect until the Russian Revolution of 1917. The country came to know them as the May Laws because they were published in that month of 1882.

The May Laws persecuted the Jews as an "economically harmful" people. They banned Jews from settling outside of cities and small towns, and they made it impossible for Jews to have anything to do with land or to live in agricultural districts. They even forbade the extension of existing leases on real estate. In effect, the laws set up a pale within the Pale, limiting even more the Jews' right of domicile and freedom of movement.

Before the May Laws, Jews could move from one village in the Pale to another. Now any change of residence was considered a new migration and banned. Even within the Pale, restrictions were imposed on Jews' freedom to live in four cities. Only special categories of Jews could live in Kiev, and then only within two police precincts. Similarly in the Black Sea ports of Sevastopol and Nikolayev. And the czar insisted that Yalta, the site of his summer palace, be isolated from the Jewish blight.

The May Laws were no sooner issued than more pogroms erupted. In Rostov, then in Yekaterinoslav, and in other cities and towns in that province, and finally, in Nizhni Novgorod, an ancient city outside the Pale where only a score of Jewish families lived. Of this small number nine were murdered. The government's response was to expel the survivors, capping the street pogrom with a legal pogrom.

Under an official policy of anti-Semitism, year after year the noose was drawn tighter around the Jews in regard to residence, education, and professional activity. The government's desire, it said, was "to improve the mutual relations" between the Jews and everyone else. But the effect of restriction was only to sharpen hostility. Jews were looked upon as pariahs, guilty from birth for being born Jews.

A quota system was established for Jews in the secondary schools, and soon extended to the universities and technical institutes. Two generations of Jewish children and their parents, eager for education, were anguished by the discriminatory quotas. For schools within the Pale the quota was set at 10 percent; outside the Pale it was 5 percent; and in Moscow and St. Petersburg it was 3 percent. In cities inside the Pale the Jews might number 30 to 80 percent of the total population, yet only 10 percent of them were allowed into school. At great cost, thousands of youths studied at home, with tutors or alone, until they could qualify to enter universities abroad, usually in Germany, France, or Switzerland.

Although Russian law did not prevent Jews from engaging in trade, industry, or crafts, Jewish economic activity was crippled by legal restrictions. The Pale kept the vast majority of Jews from settling in nine tenths of the empire. Only a tiny minority were privileged to live and trade anywhere. The effect was to keep millions of

Jews in poverty and prevent them from making a useful contribution to the economic growth of the country.

The doors to civil service in all branches of government were closed to Jews, nor could they teach in secondary schools. A few were allowed posts in higher education. Talented Jewish students were often promised professorships—if they would agree to be baptized.

Even those who had already managed to get a higher education saw their rights taken away. Doctors, lawyers, and technicians could engage only in private practice. State or academic posts were denied them. As emigration from Russia increased, the law imposed upon Jews collective responsibility for failure to report for conscription, and for physically unfit Jews. Other Jews had to replace them in military service. If a young Jew evaded such service, his family had to pay a fine of three hundred rubles. And "family" was interpreted to mean other relatives if the parents were unable to pay.

By 1890 there were at least 650 laws in the Russian Code which discriminated against Jews. "About 90 percent of the entire Jewish population is an insecure mass, living from day to day, in poverty and misery," said a government report. But while the czar's policy impoverished the Jews, it served to enrich the bureaucracy that administered it. From top to bottom, police and other officials took bribes offered by the persecuted as the only way to save themselves. Bribery was so common it was called the "Russian Constitution." It protected the innocent from arbitrary rule and the loss of their human rights.

Passover of 1891 began with an imperial decree taking away from Jewish artisans and army veterans the right to live in Moscow. Tens of thousands of Jews were ordered out of the city they had legally lived in for many decades. That night police raided Jewish homes, routed families out of bed, and hustled them to police stations. One witness left this account:

> Whoever failed to comply with the order of the police was subject to arrest; he would be jailed, and with criminals and all sorts of riffraff await his turn for deportation under a convoy. People sought refuge in cemeteries, during freezing weather, to escape arrest; women gave birth in railroad cars; in some instances ailing persons were brought in carts and transferred to the railroad cars on stretchers. Those who were subjected to that treatment remember in particular a certain ice-cold January night (1892). Throngs of Jews and their families with their pitiful bag and baggage had filled the Brest railroad station. Threatened by deportation and imprisonment, and failing to obtain a deferment, they decided to evacuate notwithstanding the weather. Fate was destined to play a spiteful trick on the unfortunates! According to a report of the chief of police, the governor-general ordered their deportation halted until the freezing weather had subsided— but that command was issued after the expatriation . . . About 20,000 Jews were thus forcibly banished to the Pale of Settlement.

The anti-Semitic press kept silent; the liberal editors

were censored. But refugees from Moscow who reached the United States let the world know the truth. In June two men, John B. Weber, U.S. Commissioner of Immigration, and the physician Dr. Walter Kempster, reached Russia, sent by an American committee to investigate the Moscow expulsions as well as conditions in the Pale. Shocked by what they saw, they published a report which said the Jewish situation was not going to improve, and urged the United States to make immigration easier for Russian Jews.

When the artisans were shipped out, Jewish merchants who were able to pay an annual fee of a thousand rubles had been allowed to stay. Now they too were treated like criminals. The police picked up anyone spotted with a "Semitic physiogonomy" and checked his documents. If they were not in order, he was deported at once. Rewards were offered for the capture of Jews without the right of domicile. In 1899 a new series of restrictions appeared, designed to free Moscow even of those Jews who had had the right of domicile.

In the Pale, restrictions multiplied, making it difficult or impossible for Jews to take vacations in the countryside or even to get medical treatment at certain resorts.

The government, with a single decree, wiped out the occupations of a quarter of a million Jews. The liquor trade was made a state monopoly in 1894, and the Jewish dealers, inn- and tavernkeepers lost their livelihood. Many Jews would all along have preferred a better way to earn their bread, but the government never permitted it. Now, deprived of their bare livings in village taverns, the Jews had little else to turn to.

Pauperism for Jews shot up in the last half of the 1890's. From 40 to 50 percent of the entire Jewish population was destitute and had to have public assistance for the Passover.

# 16 ZIONISTS AND BUNDISTS

How COMICAL WE WERE, HOW CHILD-ishly naïve," wrote one young Russian Jew after the pogroms of 1881. Like so many other Jewish radicals, he had thought there was no Jewish question, only a Russian question. With the spread of education, with political and social reform, the Russian question would be solved, and all other questions too, as a matter of course. Jew, Pole, Tatar, gypsy—all would lie down together like lambs.

Then out of the blue had come Elizavetgrad, with the mob howling, "Down with the kikes." And Kiev followed, and all the other horrors. "The blood runs cold in the veins when we look at the insulted and the humiliated," the young Jew wrote. "They seem only ghosts with deathly pale faces, expecting they know not what. At all levels of society, from the university intelligentsia to the ignorant peasant, a savage attitude towards Jews can be observed."

The pogroms made a profound change in the thinking of Russian Jews. Those of the middle class who had believed in the inevitability of progress, who had expected the complete emancipation of Jews and their unification with Russians, saw their dream become a nightmare. The student youth, who preached revolutionary action, had expected the liberated Russian—worker or peasant—to embrace the Jew as his brother. Instead, the Narodniks had hailed the pogroms as a popular movement deserving their support, and the liberals had shut their eyes to the assault upon the Jewish people.

But most shocked of all, wrote Pavel Axelrod in the pamphlet he never published, were the Jewish socialists.

> *The Jewish socialist intelligentsia suddenly realized that the majority of Russian society did, as a matter of fact, regard the Jews as a separate nation and that they considered all Jews—a pious Jewish worker, a petit bourgeois, a moneylender, an assimilated lawyer, a socialist prepared for prison or deportation—as kikes, harmful to Russia, whom Russia should get rid of by any and all means.*

Disappointed in Russia, many Jews longed for a homeland where they could determine their own destiny. In 1882, Leo Pinsker's pamphlet, *Auto-Emancipation*, voiced their cry. First published abroad in German, it was translated rapidly into Yiddish and Russian. Pinsker, an Odessa physician, had once believed assimilation was the answer. Now he held that the Jews were a distinctive group among the nations in whose territory they lived, a separate group that could neither assimilate nor be readily absorbed. Jews should no longer let themselves be forced to wander from one exile to another, he wrote. Rather, they should direct all their energies to acquiring a productive land as a permanent refuge. He thought either some place in the Americas or in Palestine would be acceptable for Jewish colonization.

In 1882, the first small group headed for Palestine. They were twenty-five students from Kharkov, socialists convinced by the wave of pogroms that their people were not the Russians but the Jews. That July they founded their first colony near Jaffa, naming it Rishon le Zion (The First in Zion). Others followed, as Jewish nationalism reawakened. On the theme of "Back to Zion!" Eliakum Zunser wrote poems calling on Jews to leave the poverty and despair of Eastern Europe and fashion a new life with their own hands in Israel. He helped deepen the tiny rivulet of Zionist immigration until it became a powerful flood.

Zunser typified those Jews who did not deny the gains of the Haskala but only the blind alleys it led to: assimilation and Russification. Another who joined his voice to Pinsker's was Moses Leib Lilienblum, who now returned to the Jewish community by advocating Zionism. He and Pinsker headed a society in Odessa organized to colonize Palestine. "The pogroms taught me their lesson," Lilienblum wrote. "I am convinced that our misfortune is not the lack of a general education but that we are aliens. We will still remain aliens when we will be stuffed with education as a pomegranate is with seeds." Through the efforts of such men, several colonies were established in Judea and Galilee in the 1880's and 1890's.

The sense of national renewal was stimulated both by anti-Semitism and by the model of liberal nationalism set in the West by such leaders as Mazzini. Among the oldest Jewish traditions was the idea of one day returning to the land of Israel. The societies bent on colonizing Palestine called themselves *Hoveve Zion*—"Lovers of Zion." They became a bridge between the intellectuals once alienated from Judaism and the traditionalist masses. Under Ahad Ha-Am's leadership, the movement developed a philosophy of Jewish nationalism. Ahad Ha-Am (the pen name of Asher Ginzberg, born in Kiev province in 1856) advocated a national cultural revival. He wanted a Jewish state in Palestine to serve as the spiritual center of world Jewry. Many of the younger Jewish writers were his disciples. One of them, Bialik, said Ahad Ha-Am brought them a new way of life, teaching them how to adapt their life to the upbuilding of the Jewish nation, raising the prestige of literature in their eyes, making them feel honored to be Hebrew authors.

True nationalism, said Ahad Ha-Am, is not contrary to the universal spirit. "Nationalism is a concrete form whereby the universal spirit reveals itself in every people in conformity with that people's circumstances, special needs, and historic course." The Jewish spirit could not be preserved in a ghetto and certainly not in assimilation. It could flower only in a culturally independent Jewish community in Palestine. He called for a cultural renaissance in the Diaspora and a physical renaissance in Palestine.

The Eastern European Jews would prove to be the mainstay of the Zionist movement. Russian Jews migrated first and most eagerly, then Galician Jews, and finally the Polish. Russia held by far the greatest number of Jews. There were now about 4 million in the Pale, 1.3

million in Congress Poland, and some 900,000 in Galicia and Bukovina. Another, much greater stream of emigration, went west, to the United States.

But it must be remembered that the vast majority of Jews stayed in Eastern Europe. And in the mass, they remained attached to their traditional faith. Pogroms and poverty were God's will, as they saw it. They had never had any illusions about the world outside the shtetl or ever considered assimilation seriously. The changes which took place now in Jewish thought sprang not from them but mostly from Jews no longer satisfied with Orthodoxy's denial of the modern world. The search for new directions came from the modernists. They wanted neither the ghetto nor assimilation, but national self-assertion. And while they scouted for the right path, they did not forget the signposts put up on the ancient road of the past.

Alexander III died in this transition period and was succeeded by Nicholas II in 1894. Nicholas was a little man in stature and character, a spineless, scheming despot. Any liberal who dreamed that a new czar on the throne would mean a constitution for Russia was at once disillusioned. Nicholas announced, "I intend to safeguard the principle of autocratic rule as steadfastly and unflinchingly as was the case with my unforgettable father." The same reactionaries remained at the key posts of government; the same anti-Jewish practices continued.

Russia had just moved into the age of big industry, a change that affected the Jews too, of course. A small upper class among them had grown wealthy through their roles as bankers, wholesalers, manufacturers, railroad builders. But the mass of Jewish workers were handicraftsmen, unable to compete with machine production. Legal restrictions, prejudice, or Sabbath observance made it hard for them to find factory jobs except in Jewish enterprises. These had grown up chiefly in Poland and Lithuania. They made but few products, and because most of them were small-scale, wages and working conditions were bad.

In his book *The Brothers Ashkenazi*, I. J. Singer pictures the rise of Jewish-owned textile factories in Poland. A few Jewish pioneers had opened a path into the weaving trade of Lodz and Jewish looms became common. Jews from the countryside around swarmed into the industry.

> *Fathers brought their sons in from the villages to learn the trade. Barefoot they came on all the roads leading into Lodz. They came with sticks in their hands to beat off the village dogs, and on the outskirts of the town they put on their boots, which they had been carrying all the way. It was the custom to apprentice the boys for three years. A sum of money, the savings and scrapings of God knew how many seasons, was paid into the hand of the master weaver. The boys would receive no pay during the apprenticeship. They would get their meals and a place to sleep in, and from morning to night they would learn.*
>
> *They stood in the hundreds at their looms, their skull-caps on their heads, the ritual fringes hanging over their cheap canvas trousers, pieces of colored*

# UN DU AKERST, UN DU ZEYST

STRUGGLE SONG

Un du a-kerst, un du zeyst,— Un du fi-terst un du neyst,

Un du ha-merst un du shpinst, Zog mayn folk vos du far-dinst?—

Refrain:

Kling klang,— Kling klang,— klapt der ha-mer mit

1.

zayng ge-zang!— Tse-rayst di key-tn fun shkla-fn tsvang!

2.

| | |
|---|---|
| Un du akerst, un du zeyst, | *You plow and you sow,* |
| Un du fiterst un du neyst, | *You tend the flock and you sew.* |
| | |
| Un du hamerst un du shpinst, | *You hammer and you spin,* |
| Zog mayn folk vos du fardinst? | *Tell me, my people, what is your gain?* |
| | |
| Vebst dayn vebshtul tog un nacht, | *You weave at the loom night and day,* |
| Grobst undz ayzn fun der shacht, | *You dig in the mine for ore,* |
| Brengst di shefa undz arayn, | *You fill the horn of plenty* |
| Ful mit t'vue un mit vayn. | *Full of wheat and wine.* |
| | |
| Nor vu iz dayn tish gegreyt? | *But where is your table spread?* |
| Nor vu iz dayn yontev kleyd? | *And where is your festive dress?* |
| Nor vu iz dayn sharfe shverd? | *Tell me, where is your sharp sword?* |
| | |
| Velches glik iz dir bashert? | *And what joy is yours to share?* |

*thread clinging to their curly hair and sprouting beards, while their hands flew swiftly over the looms, weaving from before sunrise till long after sunset the piece goods which were to be made into dresses and women's kerchiefs. As they worked they sang snatches from the synagogue services, trilling the bravura passages like real cantors, pausing with special joy on the sacred words of the high festivals. The master weavers paraded up and down the aisles, keeping an eye on the heaps of merchandise, urging the workers on, infuriated if one of them stopped to wipe the perspiration from his forehead or to roll himself a cigarette.*

The chimneys of Lodz poisoned the air, and the cesspools formed near each factory poisoned the ground. Sickness was everywhere.

*Children suffered from rickets, fathers from tuberculosis, mothers from the strain of frequent childbirth, all from undernourishment and malnutrition. The streets were almost as thick as the factories with the wool and cotton dust which came out of the looms, or, more heavily, from the rags which were being reconverted into thread. Medical service of a sort was, when obtainable, free; but medicines cost money; and the weavers dreaded having to go into the clean shiny apothecary's, with its picture of the Madonna and its glittering carboys. Here they could not haggle; they had to come in, hat in hand, take what was given, pay humbly, and crawl out.*

Low wages jammed families into one or two rooms. Rent came first—if they didn't pay, they were put out on the street at once—then food, and last of all, clothing, which meant the weavers wore nothing but rags. And when the boss cut wages? The older weavers, beaten down over the years, took it in silence. Their wives cursed and screamed. The young workers, too, were afraid.

Nevertheless, the Jewish workers did learn to organize. Workers' circles were formed, with each member paying dues. Week by week they accumulated funds to build their movement. Organizers brought them news of how workers lived in other lands. Of the international socialist movement, of the constant struggle with bosses in other parts of Eastern Europe, and of the Marxist theories which were penetrating Russia. The workers discovered their dignity and strength, and began to assert their rights. After years of struggle, as Singer points out, great changes could be seen.

> Crowds gathered everywhere fearlessly, ignoring the police and their armed attendants. The workmen's circles were well organized, and worked day and night. Their membership had grown beyond all expectation and included every class of worker: weavers, shoemakers, leather-workers, stocking-knitters, cobblers, irreligious Jews in modern clothes, religious Jews in long gaberdines, women in wigs and women who had refused to shear off their hair after marriage, but wore a red kerchief about their heads. Meetings were in

*progress everywhere, councils met, strikes were called, literature was distributed openly, speakers addressed the crowds in the streets.*

The workers' circles had become centers of the city's life.

*Apprentices came before them to complain of ill-treatment at the hands of their employers, or denounce their employers' wives for feeding them mouldy bread and sugarless coffee; housewives reported that they had been thrown out of their homes for non-payment of rent; servant girls asked for redress when their meager wages were not paid them on time. The Unionists, as the workers' leaders were called everywhere, because of their ceaseless appeals for united action, became general advisers to the working-class population. Wives of truckdrivers came to lodge complaints against drunken husbands who did not bring home their pay, but spent it in drink; there were even couples who came with their marital difficulties and turned the workers' circles into domestic-relations courts.*

The Unionists learned, and learned fast, to be effective. Day after day they did their job on the streets.

*Quick decisions were rendered, strikes called, delegates elected, ultimatums drawn up to be delivered to recalcitrant bosses. Committees were even sent with threats of direct action against profiteering grocery stores. Other committees were sent out to make the rounds of all the shops and to see to it that none of the clerks was kept after hours. Here, too, levies were assessed, and collectors sent round to shops and employers with a demand for the sum decided on.*

*No one dared to fight back. The workers' circles were all-powerful at this time . . . There was no appeal from their decision, and there was no way of bribing them; they listened to no arguments, and they could not be cited before the courts for any attempt to call in the authorities would have meant exposing oneself to the concerted vengeance of the entire workers' movement.*

Toward the end of the 1890's, this new Jewish proletariat included over 500,000 artisans, 100,000 day laborers, and 50,000 factory workers. In the light industries, where they were concentrated, the Jewish artisans far outnumbered the non-Jews. In 1897 several groups of Jewish workers, meeting in Vilna, combined into a central organization called the General Jewish Workers' Union of Lithuania, Poland, and Russia. It became known as the Bund. It grew into a powerful force in Jewish life. At first, its struggle was economic, for higher wages and shorter working hours. It soon became clear that the results could not be great. Most of the Jews worked in small shops belonging to poor artisans who themselves worked. Under the abnormal conditions of Jewish economy in the Pale, it was a strange class struggle. The Yiddish poet Abraham Liessin called it a war of "the poverty-stricken against the indigent."

In reality, both were being oppressed by the same regime, denied their civil rights, denied freedom of movement and choice of employment. The economic struggle, then, could not be separated from the political struggle against czarist autocracy.

It was through the Bund that many alienated Jews found their way back to their own people and culture. They experienced a double consciousness: of themselves as exploited workers, wanting to fight alongside their brothers for a better life, and of themselves as Jews. The early Bundist leaders felt a special responsibility toward the working class of their own people. But there were Jews active in the broader Russian socialist movement— Trotsky is an example—who regarded nationalism as reactionary and bourgeois. Such nationalism, they said, was against the principles of scientific socialism and would wreck working-class unity. The Marxists did, however, recognize the need for a separate organization of Jewish workers. Propaganda could reach them only in Yiddish, and they did have special political demands because of legal restrictions against them. When the Russian Social-Democratic Party was founded in 1898, the Bund became a part of it. Though the Russian party leaders opposed it, the Bund began to express the natural Jewish feelings of its members and to champion Jewish culture. It spoke to Jewish workers as Jews, in Yiddish, the tongue familiar to them. The *Workers' Voice* appeared as the first underground newspaper in Russia published in Yiddish. Gradually the Bund educated the workers who had grown up in the Pale, and broadened their cultural horizons. It organized a system of secular Jewish schools, with Yiddish as the language of instruction. The Bund ardently supported Yiddish literature, printing the work of its poets and novelists in its underground press. Its schools supported a Jewish cultural autonomy and stressed such traditional Jewish values as social justice. Trade unionism, politics, literature—all fused into a national Jewish revival.

Zionism too began to combine socialism with nationalism. Several socialist-Zionist groups emerged, appealing like the Bund to the Jewish working class. One of their leaflets in Lvov read:

*Jewish workers of all countries unite behind the banner of Poale Zion! Brothers and sisters of the workers' class! We see before us two great and powerful movements: on the one hand socialism which seeks to liberate us from economic and political slavery; and on the other hand Zionism which seeks to liberate us from the yoke of the Diaspora. Both affect us greatly. Both promise us a glorious future. Both are vital for us as life itself . . .*

The Bundists wanted the Jews to be able to control their own schools, their own press, their own arts. The Zionists insisted upon their own country. They differed, too, on the question of language. Which should it be—Yiddish or Hebrew? Bundists insisted upon Yiddish, the mother tongue of the Jewish masses, as the language in which children should be taught. Zionists wanted Hebrew and organized Hebrew-speaking circles to prepare the Jews in the Diaspora for the exodus to Palestine.

Although they quarreled over ideology and language, Bundists and socialist Zionists were alike in one important respect: both rejected the attitudes of accommodation or passive resistance that were traditional in the Diaspora. Both groups searched out and celebrated the ancient Jewish record of forceful resistance to persecution and slavery. No more of suffering in silence, they said. The Jewish heroes of old fought back. And so shall we.

### THE BUND HYMN

**THE OATH**
Brothers and sisters of work and need,
All who are scattered like far-flung seed—
Together! Together! The flag is high,
Straining with anger, red with blood,
So swear together to live or die!

**REFRAIN**
*Earth with its heaven hears.*
*Witness: the bright stars,*
*And our oath of blood and tears.*
*We swear. We swear.*

I
We swear to strive for freedom and right
Against the tyrant and his knave,
To best the forces of the night,
Or fall in battle, proud and brave.

II
We swear our stalwart hate persists,
Of those who rob and kill the poor:
The Czar, the Masters, Capitalists.
Our vengeance will be swift and sure.

III

To wage the holy war we vow,
Until right triumphs over wrong.
No Midas, Master, Noble now—
The humble equal to the strong.

IV

To the Bund, our hope and faith, we swear
Devotedly to set men free.
Its flag, bright scarlet, waves up there,
Sustaining us in loyalty.

*Shlomo Zanvil Rappoport (S. Ansky), 1902*

# 17 THE CITY OF SLAUGHTER

KISHINEV . . . THAT HAD BEEN ITS NAME for more than a hundred years. In 1903, the poet Bialik renamed it "The City of Slaughter."

It was the capital of the province of Bessarabia, in southwest Russia. Kishinev was noted for its gardens and orchards, so lush with fruit, and its wide streets, shaded by acacias. The town boasted a cathedral, a theological seminary, a college, a museum, and a public library. Adorning the squares were statues of Alexander II and the poet Pushkin. Its factories produced soap, candles, liquor, and tobacco. And its location on a river and a railroad made it a busy commercial center, trading in grain, wine, tobacco, tallow, wool, and skins.

About 125,000 lived in Kishinev, people of many nationalities: Moldavians, Wallachians, Russians, Bulgarians, Tatars, Germans, gypsies, and Jews.

The Jews were the largest single group, 40 percent of the town. On the eve of Passover, 1903, they became the victims of a massacre that outdid all other pogroms in savagery. Overnight obscure Kishinev became a name the whole world knew.

Kishinev had been free of the pogroms which bloodied Russian towns in the 1880's. But in 1897 the local tax collector, Krushevan, started an anti-Semitic newspaper called *Bessarabetz*. A government subsidy assured its success, and government officials wrote for it. In every issue the paper incited its readers against the Jews. It accused the Jews of capitalist exploitation of the Christians, while on the same pages it indicted the Jews as revolutionaries.

It was the only newspaper in Kishinev. The town's Jews appealed to von Plehve, the Minister of the Interior, for permission to publish another one, to counteract *Bessarabetz*. His reply was, "The *Bessarabetz* is good enough for Kishinev."

Von Plehve had long been identified by the Jews as their new Haman. A quarter of a century before, at the time of the pogroms which followed the assassination of Alexander II, he had been head of the empire's police. In 1902 Nicholas II named him Minister of the Interior to succeed Sipiagin, who had been shot by a terrorist. By now, revolutionary ferment had spread to wider circles. With the rise of an organized labor movement and new socialist parties, the revolutionists were no longer a handful but thousands of discontented men and women on all levels of society. When von Plehve was police chief there were never more than two underground printing presses at a time. Now there were more than twenty. Where a handful might have taken part in the rare street demonstrations of a generation before, now fifty thousand gathered in the squares of St. Petersburg to unfurl their red flags and listen to revolutionary speeches. May Day, the international holiday of labor, had become the great day for clashes between police and Cossacks on one side, and workers and students on the other.

Nicholas was shaken by the threat to the throne. The Jews, his advisers repeated endlessly, were at the center of the revolutionary danger. It was true that the Jews in the movement were greater in number than their proportion to the general population. But hounded and humiliated as they had been by czarism, it was no wonder. They had organized the Bund, of course, and they joined the Russian Social-Democratic and the Socialist Revolutionary Parties. When police publicly flogged Jews who took part in a Bund demonstration in Vilna on May Day, 1901, a Bundist shoemaker, Hirsh Lekert, shot the Vilna governor. He failed to kill him, and was executed. His act of vengeance was followed by the mass arrest of young Jews. Thousands were sent to prison or into Siberian exile.

Von Plehve tried to use the Jews as a tool to divert public dissatisfaction with the regime to attacks upon these "foreigners." He sought to destroy the freedom movement by labeling it a Jewish plot.

The ground had already been prepared. Back in 1895, Russians living in France had cooked up something called the *Protocols of the Elders of Zion*. This gross forgery presented itself as a conspiracy of Jews to seize world power which had been plotted and recorded at an imaginary assembly of Jewish leaders. The fabrication had reached the czar's court, adding its poison to the anti-Semitism long rampant there. To Nicholas II "Jew" and "enemy" became interchangeable words. He called any-one who opposed him a Jew. Plehve's plan "to drown the revolution in Jewish blood" easily won czarist ap-proval.

The regime promoted the belief that the Jews were harmful to the state and to the people. Officials, police, military, ordinary citizens absorbed the idea that the Jews were outside the law's protection. These were "enemies" who could be abused and mistreated at will. As *Bess-arabetz* whipped up anti-Jewish feeling, the police offi-cials in Kishinev spoke openly of a coming day when the town would be rid of the Jews. Leaflets showered the streets proclaiming that a czarist edict permitted the slaughter of the Jews during Easter.

That Easter Sunday—it was April 6, 1903, and it hap-pened to fall on the last day of Passover—the church bells rang at noon. As if by signal, gangs flooded the streets and began to beat up any Jews they encountered. The police and militia stood by, doing nothing. Their inaction convinced the pogromists that they had official approval. Crying "Kill the Jews!" the rapidly swelling mob rushed into the Jewish streets, breaking into homes and shops, smashing furniture, stealing money and goods, and beating up anyone who protested.

By late afternoon the drunken rabble armed with clubs and axes were killing Jews in their homes and on the streets. Still the authorities were silent. At 10 p.m. the pogrom halted. Some Jews rallied to defend them-selves, but when they appeared on the streets with clubs, the police disarmed them.

Now the rioters controlled the town. A report described what followed:

> On Monday from 3 a.m. until 8 p.m., mobs raged in
> the midst of the desolation and ruin which they had
> themselves heaped; they plundered, robbed, and de-
> stroyed Jewish property; they stole, pillaged, and
> spoiled; they hounded, assaulted, abused, and tortured
> Jewish persons. Representatives of all classes of the
> population participated in this frightful witches' Sab-
> bath: soldiers and police, officials and priests, children
> and women, peasants, workers, tramps.

A Jewish delegation asked the governor of Bessarabia
for help. He replied that the military—there were five
thousand troops in the garrison—could not move without orders from St. Petersburg. Not until five o'clock
that Monday afternoon did Plehve telegraph the order.
The soldiers came out on the streets, and without a shot
being fired, the mob melted away. But on the outskirts
of town the looting and terror continued until Tuesday
morning.

The toll: 45 murdered, 86 seriously injured, 500 less
seriously hurt, 1,500 homes and shops plundered or destroyed, and 10,000 left homeless and penniless. The victims were chiefly the poor—artisans and small shopkeepers. The wealthy families were able to bribe the
police to protect them.

Bialik was sent to Kishinev by the Jews of Odessa who
wanted to know exactly what had happened there. In-

stead of producing a routine report, Bialik wrote a powerful prophetic poem, "The City of Slaughter":

*She saw it all, and she's a living witness,*
*The old gray spider spinning in the garret.*
*She knows a lot of stories—bid her tell them!*
*A story of a belly stuffed with feathers,*
*Of nostrils and of nails, of heads and hammers,*
*Of men, who, after death, were hung head downward,*
*Like these, along the rafter.*
*A story of a suckling child asleep,*
*A dead and cloven breast between its lips,*
*And of another child they tore in two,*
*And many, many more such fearful stories*
*That beat about the head and pierce thy brain,*
*And stab the soul within thee, does she know.*

The rage felt by the Jew of Russia was in those lines, rage against those guilty of the massacre. But shame too, shame for the Jews who had given up their lives without resistance. In his poem, Bialik goes on to express that feeling:

*Can you hear? They beat their breasts, "Forgive us!"*
*They call to Me I should forgive their sins!*
*How sins a shadow on the wall, a dead worm?*
*A broken pitcher?*
*Why do they pray? Why do they lift their hands?*
*Where is their fist? Where is the thunderbolt*
*That would settle accounts for all the generations*

*And lay the world in ruins, tear down heavens,*
*and overturn My Throne! . . .*
*Your unwept tear bury within you,*
*Immure it in your heart, build up there*
*Of hate and wrath and gall for it a fortress,*
*And let it grow, a serpent in its nest,*
*And you will suckle from each other,*
*Yet always hungering and thirsty you will be.*
*Then when the evil day comes upon you,*
*Break your heart open, liberate the snake.*
*And like a poisoned arrow send it*
*Ravenous, with burning venom,*
*Into the very heart of your own people.*

The pogrom at Kishinev roused non-Jewish writers to voice their disgust with the behavior of a society that called itself Christian. Maxim Gorky said in a public letter:

*The mob, merely the hand which was guided by a corrupt conscience, driving it to murder and robbery, was led by men of cultured society. But cultivated society in Russia is really much worse than the people who are goaded by their sad life and blinded and enthralled by the artificial darkness created around them . . . Cultivated society is not less guilty of the disgraceful and horrible deeds committed at Kishinev than the actual murderers and ravishers. Its members' guilt consists in the fact that, not merely did they not protect the victim, but that they rejoiced over the murders; it consists chiefly in committing themselves for long years to be corrupted by man-haters and persons who have long enjoyed the disgusting glory of being the lackeys of power and the glorifiers of lies.*

Tolstoy, who had been silent during the pogroms of the 1880's, now wrote:

*After the first reports in the newspapers, I understood the entire horror of what had occurred, and sensed simultaneously deep commiseration with the innocent victims of the ruthlessness of the population, consternation over the atrocities of so-called Christians, repugnance toward those so-called cultured people, who incited the mob and sympathized with their actions. I was dismayed in particular at the chief culprit—our government and its clergy which rouse in the people animal emotions and fanaticism, and with its gang of officials and brigands. The Kishinev crime —that is a direct result of that propaganda of falsehood and violence which our government carries on with such energy. The attitude of our government towards these events is only one more proof of the brutal egoism which does not flinch from any measures, however cruel, when it is a question of suppressing a movement which is deemed dangerous, and of their complete indifference . . . towards the most terrible outrages which do not affect government interests.*

In Russia the truth of Kishinev was concealed by official censorship. The government ordered that its version be printed by the press. Plehve's story ran that the pogrom was only the chance outcome of a squabble on the street that had been started by a Jew. But the facts hurdled over the censors and found their way into the foreign press. The newspapers of Europe and America detailed the massacre and the world reacted in horror to such inhumanity. In the light of Hitler's holocaust, Kishinev may now seem minor, but Bialik's vision was true: Kishinev was a beginning whose end would be Auschwitz.

The Jews of Russia, stunned at first by the repetition of mass murder, were galvanized into action by Bialik's scathing "The City of Slaughter." Young Jews organized defense units in many towns and villages, and armed themselves against future Kishinevs. The Jewish students at the Polytechnic Institute in Kiev, recalled Nokhum Shtif, "responded with a self-defense group and with revolutionary proclamations . . . We expanded our work, providing the region with arms. I had practically stopped studying . . ."

One of the Kiev Polytechnic students, a socialist Zionist named Pinhas Dashevsky, tried and failed to assassinate Krushevan, the editor of *Bessarabetz*, for inciting the Kishinev pogrom. Plehve concluded the Zionists too must be suppressed. Their meetings and fund raising were banned, and the police took to hounding them.

Zalman Shazar, then fifteen, had just joined Poale Zion secretly when a group was clandestinely set up in his home town. Steibtz was full of muscular Jewish laborers, and the first thing the young party did was to organize a self-defense group. Upon hearing rumors of an impending pogrom, the Jews pitched in money and bought revolvers in Minsk. The self-defense group soon numbered a hundred trained and equipped men, divided into units of ten. Word spread that an attack on the Jews was planned Sunday after church. Shazar recalled:

> We knew that instigators had come from distant places; we saw peasant women arriving with empty wagons which, it was understood, they expected to fill with the booty robbed from the Jews. From early in the morning our members were stationed in the marketplace, lead-tipped iron bars in their hands and lead-tipped leather thongs in their pockets. The heads of our groups carried concealed revolvers and divided the watch over the marketplace among themselves.
>
> At noon an agitated and excited crowd, all ready for the attack, came pouring out of the white church above the marketplace. One of the "guests" rushed to the fore, dragging the peasants after him towards the stores. At that moment all the revolvers, scattered over the marketplace, went off at once. They shot into the air and hurt no one, but even that was enough to intimidate the crowd. Bedlam ensued. The horses were frightened, the peasant women screamed as if they were being slaughtered, and the wagons collided with each other. The peasants ran with their last breath, fleeing from the armed Jews. And the revolvers kept on shooting. In a few moments the marketplace was empty . . .

Meanwhile, a court investigation of the Passover pogrom at Kishinev began. The official inquiry covered up all traces of government complicity. Only the common criminals caught on the scene—those who had wielded ax and torch—were tried and sentenced. Every attempt by lawyers to get at those who had given the commands was ruled out of order. The government also refused to accept civil suits by Jews to recover losses suffered in the pogrom.

The court was still sitting on the Kishinev crime when a pogrom exploded in Gomel, a town in the province of Mohilev, where 60 percent of the people were Jewish. A fight between Christians and Jews broke out in the marketplace on August 29, 1903, and a peasant was killed. The police arrested only Jews. Two days later a mob of railroad workers swarmed through the town, pillaging Jewish homes, shops, and synagogues. A detachment of hundreds of armed Jews began driving them back. But when the troops arrived they fired upon the Jews, killing three and wounding several others. Encouraged, the mob resumed its destruction, shielded by the soldiers from the Jewish self-defense unit. That night, when the pogrom ended, twelve Jews and eight Christians were dead or seriously wounded. Hundreds of homes and shops had been plundered.

A few days later the governor of Mohilev summoned leading Jews to the town council and said to them that Jews were to blame for leading all the movements against the government. That was why the Russian masses had turned upon them. He was echoing Plehve's line. The revolutionaries soon caught up with the Minister of the Interior. Sazonov, the son of a rich lumber merchant, expelled from Moscow University in a student strike and exiled to Siberia, turned terrorist and blew up Plehve with a bomb.

At the end of January 1904, the Russo-Japanese War began. The czarist government, with a population vastly outnumbering the Japanese, expected to win easily. But there was little popular enthusiasm for a war to annex Manchuria to Siberia.

In preparation for the war, the regime had expelled two thousand Jews from Port Arthur and the Far East peninsula. Refused the use of rail transport, the homeless Jews were forced to travel a thousand miles on foot in bitter winter. Nevertheless, the day after war was declared, *Voskhod*, a Jewish journal, wrote:

> *This is not the time to rub salt on old wounds. Let us try—inasmuch as it is in our power—to forget, both the recent expulsion from Port Arthur and the pogroms of Kishinev and Gomel, as well as much else. Let Jewish parents not meditate now over the bitter fate of their children, who were not admitted to educational institutions. Jews will go into battle as enlisted men; but the blood of our children will be shed as profusely as that of the Russians.*

Tens of thousands of Jews joined up to fight for Russian glory, even while the government continued to persecute their people. Many Jews, however, fled from military duty, and emigration to America jumped.

When the czar's armies met defeat after defeat, the

anti-Semitic press spread stories that the Jews were conniving to help the Japanese in order to avenge Kishinev. More pogroms were threatened for Easter of 1904. But in fear of internal disorders while at war, the governors were given strict orders not to allow them. None did occur that Easter—proving how easy it was for the regime to start or stop the massacres at will.

As the authorities became more brutal in their use of force, the revolutionaries became more insistent upon their demands. On the "Bloody Sunday" of January 9, 1905, the workers of St. Petersburg, led by Father Gapon, marched en masse to the Winter Palace to petition the czar for reforms. They were fired upon by the Royal Guards. The response was strikes, demonstrations, and more acts of Red terror. When the Grand Duke Sergius and others were assassinated, the czar felt he had better make some concessions. A council was appointed to draft a constitution, and recommendations were invited from the people. The Jews, divided into many political groups, hotly debated what to propose. Baron Günzburg's wealthy circle pleaded that because the Jews were useful to the state their persecution should be halted. But others would not plead: they demanded the rights due them. In April 1905 the Alliance for the Achievement of Complete Equal Rights for the Jewish People of Russia was organized. The historian Simon Dubnow, one of its founders, said that in modern times it was "the first attempt at a struggle for freedom *as a Jewish nation* rather than as a religious group."

Jews from dozens of communities followed up with petitions for equality, some adding the rights of national and cultural self-determination. The one basic reform all progressive Russians demanded was the end of autocracy and the adoption of a parliamentary constitution.

That Easter, pogroms broke out in several cities. One of them, in Zhitomir, was on the scale of a second Kishinev. It was planned by the police in conjunction with the Black Hundreds, a new organization which combined the appeals of anti-Semitism and nationalism in a way that anticipated Hitler's fascism. Crying "Attack the revolutionaries and the Jews!" a mob went into action. The police and military stood by, doing nothing to defend Jewish life or property, but interfering with the self-defense units. At the end of a two-day battle fifteen Jews and a Russian student who fought on their side were dead and sixty seriously injured. On the third day, Jews forced their way into the governor and threatened general slaughter if he did not put down the pogrom. He gave the orders and it stopped quickly.

## SONG OF THE ZHITOMIR POGROM

Efsher vilt ir, mentshn visn,
Vi der pogrom iz geven
Shabes farnacht af der
  polikovke,
Iz gefaln a chaver vi a shteyn.

Vi mir zenen in gas
  aroysgegangen,
Shrayan chuliganes: *bey
  zhidov!*
Vi mir zenen tsum
  *ploshtshadek* tsugekumen,
Gefaln iz der student blinov.

*People, perhaps you would like
  to know,
How the pogrom took place.
Saturday evening on Polikovke,
A comrade fell, like a stone.*

*As we came out into the street,
Rioters were yelling: Kill the
  Jews!
As we approached the square,
Blinov, the student, fell dead.*

Vi di kozakn zenen
  ongekumen,
Mit di *oruzhes* in di hent,
Dem ershtn vistrel hobn zey
  gegebn.
Un zhitomir af prach
  farbrent.

*As the Cossacks arrived,*
*With their guns in their hands,*
*They shot their first round of*
  *fire*
*And burned Zhitomir to the*
  *ground.*

The defeat of the Russian forces in Manchuria was followed by the Japanese victory over the Russian fleet at Tsushima in the summer of 1905. Defeated on the battlefield, the soldiers and Cossacks sought a cheap victory on the streets, killing as many as fifty Jews in Bialystok alone.

With the country torn apart by revolutionary and counterrevolutionary demonstrations, the government finally issued a draft constitution in August. There would be elections to a Duma or parliament which would have only advisory status. Jews would be allowed to vote and run for office, although they were still denied other elementary rights. Not satisfied with a token gesture, workers and students began fresh rounds of strikes that would build up to a great all-Russia general strike designed to force a truly democratic constitution upon the czar. The Black Hundreds made their plans at the same time and clashes between the two opposing forces became bloodier and more frequent. At last the government seemed ready to yield to the democratic movement. On October 17 an imperial manifesto promised full civil rights and a democratically elected Duma with legislative powers. However, the czar made no promise of equality for all citizens or for all nationalities.

Victims of a pogrom, photographed in March 1919

*The Bettmann Archive*

The next day the Black Hundreds responded with a blood bath that protracted its horrors for a full week: large or smaller pogroms erupted in more than seven hundred cities, towns, and villages, in the Pale and even beyond it.

It was a counterrevolution—planned, systematic, ruthless. In each locality the same pattern: it began as a patriotic parade to celebrate the czar's manifesto, with marchers carrying his portrait. Invariably the portrait was fired upon by persons unknown. It was shouted that Jews had done the shooting, and on this signal an anti-Jewish riot was begun. Plehve had once said, "I will choke the revolution in the blood of the Jews." It was estimated that in one week 900 Jews were murdered, leaving 325 widows and 1,350 orphans, and more than 8,000 were injured. Thousands of homes, synagogues, and shops were destroyed. More than 200,000 Jews were in one way or another victims of the pogroms. Later, two of the Jewish deputies to the first Duma were murdered by the Black Hundreds.

The worst pogrom that week was Odessa's. It lasted four days, and left 302 dead (fifty-five of them members of the self-defense group), 5,000 wounded, 1,400 businesses ruined, 3,000 artisans reduced to beggary, and 40,000 homeless. Mendele Mocher Sforim, who lived in Odessa and was nearly seventy at the time of the pogrom, was asked by a Swiss socialist paper to write about it. He refused because he could not disguise his feelings or use Aesopian language. And if he should say what he truly thought, it would mean exile to Siberia.

> *If I should now write, my heart would flare and my*
> *blood would boil . . . I must not do this, as I cannot*
> *remain an emigrant and I am too old for exile . . . I,*
> *an old man, have in the days of the pogrom in Odessa*
> *hid in the janitor's pigsty. Like a pig I lay hidden!*
> *Instead of taking hold of an axe and splitting their*
> *heads—I crawled away and hid for days—like a pig! I*
> *cannot write about that! If I should sit down to write I*
> *would not be able to keep from writing something*
> *that would become my "act of accusation" to send me*
> *to exile.*

Both the left and the more moderate democratic groups felt the czar had betrayed them. With one hand he had given the promise of a constitutional system, and with the other he had stabbed them in the back. His treachery brought the country to the boiling point. Assemblies, conferences, strikes took place by the hundreds. The tumult of the earlier underground days now rose to the surface of public life.

The Jewish Federation for Equal Rights met in St. Petersburg that November and made plans to direct all its efforts to organizing Russian Jewry for self-defense. The Jews would no longer beg. "We will not accept equal rights from the bloody hands of the autocracy," one young delegate cried out. "We will accept them from a free Russian parliament!" A few months later the federation met again to plan for the election of Jews to the Duma. A left-wing minority wanted to boycott the elections, but the majority decided it was better to participate in them. The goal was to elect Jewish candidates wherever possible, and in other places to vote for a non-Jew if he would promise to support the civil, political, and national rights of the Jewish people.

Of the 497 deputies elected, twelve were Jews, six of them Zionists. One of the twelve was Shmarya Levin. Born in Swislocz in 1867, he had become a Zionist in his youth. In his autobiography he describes the first meeting of the Duma in May 1906:

> I was elected almost unanimously as the representative of Vilna to the first Russian Duma. There were twelve of us in all, the representatives of between six and seven million Jews, and I wonder whether any twelve men have ever carried upon their shoulders the responsibility of so many hopes and longings. Russia was—so it seemed—about to rise out of the abyss of oppression; the Jewish people was about to rise out of an abyss below the abyss, and these twelve men were to haul it out. To make their task harder, these men had to bear in mind that they had been elected by non-Jewish as well as by Jewish voters, and frequently there was no correspondence between the work they had to do for their own people and the party needs dictated by their other constituencies . . .
>
> Among the Jewish deputies, I occupied, in a certain sense, a special position, not for my virtues or abilities, but because of one of those fantastic anomalies which are so frequent in Russian Jewish life. I was the only one among them who had no right to stay in St.

*Petersburg. The others belonged, one way or another, to the class of the "privileged" Jews, either by academic association, or through their standing in the business guilds. But my degree.had been taken at a foreign university, and I was no businessman. I was therefore one of the six million who could not leave the Pale. And so I walked around in St. Petersburg as the living symbol of the absurd system, as if to say: "I have no right to be living in St. Petersburg at all, and I am only here for the purpose of helping to make the country's laws." I did not neglect to point this out . . . in the Duma.*

While the Duma was debating the government's role in the pogroms of 1905, a pogrom broke out in Bialystok. Soldiers joined in with the mob and shot Jews down for hours. Eighty were killed and hundreds wounded in a massacre that exceeded most others for bestiality—limbs chopped off, nails driven into heads, bellies ripped open, children's brains knocked out. When the bloody news reached St. Petersburg, Levin said:

*A tremor went through the Duma. It was not only the pogrom as such, but the hint that it contained . . . The Duma resolved at once to send a commission of investigation to the actual scene . . . The Bialystok pogrom had acted like a cold shower on Jews and liberal Russians alike, and many had begun to feel that the Duma would not live much longer. Among the Jews, the depression was of course at its worst.*

The commission finished its inquiry into Bialystok and returned:

> *Fiery speeches were delivered in the Duma by Vinaver, Jacubson and Rodichev [Jewish deputies]. By an overwhelming majority the Duma accepted a resolution calling upon the Czar to dismiss his Cabinet, in order that the rulers of the country might dissociate themselves from the disgrace of the pogrom. The atmosphere, during the debate, was heavily charged. The deputies knew that they now stood at the parting of the ways. Two days later, when they turned up at the chamber, they found the doors locked and guarded. Outside was posted the manifesto of the Czar dissolving the Duma.*

His excuse was that the Duma had gone beyond its authority in land reform and had investigated acts of the government—meaning pogroms. A Second Duma was elected, this time with only four Jewish deputies. It too had a short and fruitless life. When it was dissolved, the government arbitrarily changed the electoral law. It gave far more voting power to the landowners and the propertied city classes than was their due. The effect was to make the Third (1907–12) and Fourth (1913–15) Dumas the instrument of the reactionaries. The Black Hundreds were able to put through more and even worse laws against the Jews.

# Afterword

World War I brought wild changes in Europe. The losses in life were enormous. The chief battleground of the war in the Eastern zone turned out to be the homelands of the Jews. "As Imperial Russia's army advanced," wrote the historian Lucy Dawidowicz, "it arrested, tortured, deported, and massacred the Jews; retreating, the Russians repeated the process. Six times the Russians advanced into Galicia and Bukovina, and six times they retreated. Many Poles assisted the Russians in tormenting the Jews, as many were later to assist the Nazi Germans. During 1915, the Germans occupied Congress Poland and most of the Pale and inaugurated a systematic and orderly economic exploitation of resources and labor which, on top of the war ravages, pauperized the Jewish population. Hunger, disease, and destitution were the common Jewish condition . . ."

With the Russian Revolution of 1917 came the hope of peace, of civil rights, of cultural autonomy for the Jews. The Revolution made Jews full citizens and abolished all restrictions upon them. But the civil war that followed drowned Jewish hopes in a bloody wave of pogroms. When the Red Army triumphed, assuring the rule of the Communist Party over Russia, anti-Semitism was made a crime. After so many centuries, Russian Jews were for the first time declared the equal of their fellow countrymen. What happened to Russia's Jews in the generations since 1917 is another story. As for the rest of Eastern Europe, rightist governments or fascist dictatorships eventually took control of the newly independent nations after World War I and the Jews were always among their first victims.

With the rise of Germany under Hitler and the outbreak of World War II came the holocaust. Six million Jews were murdered. Of Poland's 3.25 million Jews, 3 million were killed. Today in Eastern Europe there are about 3 million Jews, most of them living in the Soviet Union. (Another 2.6 million Jews are in Israel.)

Apart from these survivors, the Jews who escaped death in the wars, revolutions, and mass slaughter were the Jews who began leaving Eastern Europe in the 1880's. In the thirty years following Alexander II's assassination, one out of every three Jews in Eastern Europe fled from its poverty and persecution. By the end of the 1920's, when immigration had been almost shut off, 3.25 million Jews had entered the United States. Today they and their descendants make up the vast majority of America's 6 million Jews.

Their story is in some ways like that of the many other white ethnic groups who immigrated to the New World. But in many important aspects it is quite different and deserves a book unto itself.

# Glossary

The Yiddish words used in this book are usually explained when they are introduced. Nevertheless, a glossary may prove useful to some readers. There is great variation in the transliteration of Yiddish words. In the quotations used, the same word may be spelled differently from text to text. To prevent confusion, I have taken the liberty of changing the spelling in sources quoted to make them conform to my arbitrary choice. The glossary follows those choices. Pronunciation, too, varies, so I have not attempted to impose a standard that does not exist. If you do not know how to say a word, ask!

BAGEL   A hard roll, shaped like a doughnut, simmered in hot water for two minutes before baking, then glazed with egg white.

BENTSH LICHT   To recite the blessing over Sabbath or holiday candles.

BOKHER   A boy.

BORSHT   Beet soup.

BUND   General Jewish Workers' Union of Lithuania, Poland, and Russia.

CABALA   Jewish mystical movement. The body of Jewish mystical tradition, literature, and thought.

CHALLAH   A braided loaf of white bread, glazed with egg white, and delicious.

CHANUKAH The Feast of Dedication or Lights, commemorating the victory of the Jewish Maccabees over the Syrians in a fight for religious freedom, 167 B.C.

CHEDER Elementary religious school.

DALLUS Poverty.

DIASPORA Exile. Dispersion of the Jews among the lands outside of Israel.

DYBBUK Evil spirit, usually a condemned soul that gets hold of a living person on whom the dead one has a claim.

GAN ADEN The Garden of Eden.

GAON Genius. Originally title given to heads of Babylon's rabbinical academy. Applied to rabbi of exceptional learning.

GEMARA One of the two basic parts of the Talmud. It interprets and discusses the law as presented in the other part, the Mishnah.

GESHEFT Business.

GEZUNT Health.

GOY Anyone not a Jew. A Gentile.

HAGGADAH The historical narrative read aloud at the Passover seder, incorporating psalms, prayers, and songs. It tells the story of Israel's bondage in, and flight from, Egypt.

HASID Follower or member of the Hasidic movement.

HASIDISM Religious movement founded by Israel Baal Shem Tov in the seventeenth century.

HASKALA Enlightenment. The movement for intellectual emancipation, for secularization of Jewish life.

KADDISH The mourner's prayer.

KAHAL Congregation, community. Jewish community organization.

KEHILLA Congregation or community. The organization of the community.

KHIDDUSH   Prayer or ceremony sanctifying the Sabbath and Jewish holy days.

KHUMESH   The Pentateuch, the five books of Moses.

KNISH   Small dumpling stuffed with groats, grated potatoes, chopped liver, onions, or cheese.

KOP   Head.

KOSHER   Food ritually fit to eat because prepared under the dietary laws.

KUGEL   Pudding of noodles or potatoes.

LAG B'OMER   Mid-spring harvest holiday.

LITVAK   A Lithuanian Jew.

LUFTMENSCH   A dreamer (airman) without an occupation, who makes a living from who knows what.

MALOCHIM   Angels.

MANDLEN   Almonds.

MASKIL   A follower of the Haskala, an enlightened one.

MATZO   Unleavened bread eaten during Passover.

MELAMED   Teacher, usually of elementary Hebrew.

MIDRASH   The analysis and exposition of the Holy Scriptures.

MISHNAH   That basic part of the Talmud which is the codified Oral Law.

MISNAGID   One opposed to Hasidism.

MITZVA   Divine commandment. Good deed, meritorious act.

MOHEL   Circumciser.

MOSERIM   Informers.

PARNOSSEH   Livelihood, occupation, trade.

PENTATEUCH   The five books of Moses, which begin the Old Testament.

PILPUL   A complicated scholarly analysis or interpretation of a rabbinical text.

PROSTEH   The simple, the common. Unschooled or lower-class Jews.

REBBE   Teacher; title given a learned man. Used as equivalent of mister.

SANHEDRIN   The seventy elders, headed by a patriarch, who sat in Jerusalem until A.D. 70 as a kind of Supreme Court, ruling on theological, ethical, civil, and political questions.

SCHWER   Hard.

SEDER   The festive meal and religious service held on the first and second evenings of Passover.

SEYKHEL   Intelligence, good sense.

SHABBOS   Sabbath.

SHEYDIM   Ghosts, devils, evil spirits.

SHEYNEH   The beautiful, the fine. Upper-class Jews.

SHOCHET   Ritual slaughterer.

SHOLEM   Peace. Health. Hello.

SHTADLAN   One who uses his influence with the authorities on behalf of the community.

SHTETL   Village, small town, especially the Jewish communities of Eastern Europe before World War II.

SHUL   Synagogue.

SHULKHAN ARUKH   Title of compendium of rabbinical law, by Joseph Caro.

SUCCOTH   The Festival of Tabernacles, or Feast of Booths, a harvest holiday.

TALLIS   Prayer shawl worn by male Jews during prayers.

TALMUD   Basic compendium of Jewish law based upon scholarly interpretation of the Torah. A monumental body of many books.

TORAH   The first five books of the Old Testament, known as the Five Books of Moses: Genesis, Exodus, Leviticus, Numbers, and Deuteronomy. All Jewish law and wisdom.

TSADIK   A saint. A righteous one. A Hasidic leader.

VELT   World.

VOKH   Week.

YESHIVA    Rabbinical college or seminary.

YICHUS    Status, based on learning, wealth, ancestry, or relatives.

ZADDIK    Righteous man, holy man, possibly with supernatural powers.

ZMIROS    Songs recited after the Sabbath meal.

# Bibliography and Acknowledgments

I came to this work severely handicapped by my inability to read Hebrew and Yiddish. Much of the source materials on the antecedents of American Jewry are to be found only in those languages. I owe thanks all the more, therefore, to the Yivo Institute for Jewish Research and to its librarian, Dina Abramowicz, for guiding me to what was available in English in that incomparable collection.

Among the many scholars to whom I am indebted, three especially must be singled out: Mark Zborowski and Elizabeth Herzog for their pioneering study of the shtetl, *Life Is with People,* and Lucy S. Dawidowicz for her book, *The Golden Tradition: Jewish Life and Thought in Eastern Europe.* I mined both works mercilessly, and must give extra thanks to Ms. Dawidowicz for her translations of many Yiddish texts. My grateful appreciation at the same time to all the other translators from the Yiddish and the Hebrew whose work is too often ill-paid and unacknowledged. (I wish some Rothschild would endow the translation of the large number of Yiddish works which yet remain to be put into English.)

The best way for a reader to go deeper into the world of East European Jewry is to read its literature—the short stories, sketches, novels, plays, memoirs, letters, poems, essays, speeches. It was to such original sources that I went to discover how it felt to be a Jew in the Eastern Europe my mother and father came from. These eyewitness accounts give us a human passage to the past, and I have used them liberally in my narrative.

For one unfamiliar with the literature, there are good guides to follow: Maurice Samuel's *The World of Sholem Aleichem*, his book about I. L. Peretz, *Prince of the Ghetto*, and the two collections of Yiddish material made by Irving Howe and Eliezer Greenberg, illuminated by their superb historical introductions.

The sources listed below are a selection of the books and articles I referred to in my research. I also made frequent use of the files of contemporary newspapers and periodicals, and of historical journals found either at Yivo or in the Judaica collection of the New York Public Library.

ABRAHAMS, ISRAEL, *Jewish Life in the Middle Ages*. London: Goldston, 1932.

ABRAMOVITCH, HIRSCH, "Rural Jewish Occupations in Lithuania." *Yivo Annual of Jewish Social Sciences*, Vols. II–III, (1947–8), pp. 205–21. New York: Yiddish Scientific Institute-Yivo.

AIN, ABRAHAM, "Swislocz. Portrait of a Jewish Community in Eastern Europe." *Yivo Annual of Jewish Social Sciences*, Vol. IV (1949), pp. 86–114. New York: Yiddish Scientific Institute-Yivo.

ANTIN, MARY, *The Promised Land*. Boston: Houghton Mifflin, 1969.

BARON, SALO W., *A Social and Religious History of the Jews*, 3 vols. New York: Columbia University Press, 1937.

BEN-SASSON, H. H., and Ettinger, S., eds., *Jewish Society Through the Ages*. New York: Schocken Books, 1971.

BILLINGTON, JAMES H., *The Icon and the Axe, an Interpretive History of Russian Culture*. New York: Alfred A. Knopf, 1966.

BROSS, JACOB, "The Beginning of the Jewish Labor Movement in Galicia." *Yivo Annual of Jewish Social Sciences*, Vol. V (1950), pp. 55–84. New York: Yiddish Scientific Institute-Yivo.

BUBER, MARTIN, *Origin and Meaning of Hasidism*. New York: Horizon Press, 1960.

CAHAN, ABRAHAM, *The Education of Abraham Cahan*. Philadelphia: Jewish Publication Society, 1969.

———, "Jewish Massacres and the Revolutionary Movement in Russia." *North American Review*, Vol. 77 (July 1903), pp. 49–62.

CHARNOFSKY, MICHAEL, *Jewish Life in the Ukraine*. New York: Exposition Press, 1965.

COHEN, MORRIS R., *A Dreamer's Journey*. New York: Free Press, 1949.

DAVITT, MICHAEL, *Within the Pale*. Philadelphia: Jewish Publication Society, 1903.

DAWIDOWICZ, LUCY S., ed., *The Golden Tradition: Jewish Life and Thought in Eastern Europe*. New York: Holt, Rinehart and Winston, 1967.

DIMONT, MAX I., *Indestructible Jews*. New York: New American Library, 1971.

———, *Jews, God and History*. New York: New American Library, 1962.

DUBNOW, SIMON, *History of the Jews: From the Congress of Vienna to the Emergence of Hitler*, Vol. 5. New York: Thomas Yoseloff, 1973.

———, *History of the Jews in Russia and Poland*. Philadelphia: Jewish Publication Society, 1916–20.

ELBOGEN, ISMAR, A *Century of Jewish Life, 1840–1940*. Philadelphia: Jewish Publication Society, 1944.

FINKELSTEIN, LOUIS, ed., *The Jews*, 3 vols. New York: Schocken Books, 1971.

FLANNERY, EDWARD H., *The Anguish of the Jews: Twenty-three Centuries of Anti-Semitism*. New York: Macmillan, 1965.

FRUMKIN, JACOB; Aronson, Gregor; and Goldenwieser, Alexis, *Russian Jewry, 1860–1917*. New York: Thomas Yoseloff, 1966.

GORDON, BENJAMIN LEE, *Between Two Worlds*. New York: Bookman, 1952.

GRAYZEL, SOLOMON, A *History of the Contemporary Jews: From 1900 to the Present*. New York: Atheneum, 1972.

———, A *History of the Jews*. Philadelphia: Jewish Publication Society, 1962.

HARCAVE, SIDNEY, *Years of the Golden Cockerel: The Last Romanov Tsars, 1814–1917*. New York: Macmillan, 1968.

HESCHEL, ABRAHAM J., *The Earth Is the Lord's: The Inner World of the Jew in East Europe*. New York: Schuman, 1950.

HOWE, IRVING, and Greenberg, Eliezer, eds., A *Treasury of Yiddish Stories*. New York: Meridian, 1958.

———, *Voices from the Yiddish*. Ann Arbor: University of Michigan Press, 1972.

LAQUEUR, WALTER, A *History of Zionism*. New York: Holt, Rinehart and Winston, 1972.

LIPTZIN, SOL, *Eliakum Zunser: Poet of His People*. New York: Behrman House, 1950.

LISITZKY, E. E., *In the Grip of Cross-Currents*. New York: Exposition Press, 1959.

MADISON, CHARLES, *Yiddish Literature: Its Scope and Major Writers*. New York: Schocken Books, 1971.

MARCUS, JACOB R., ed., *The Jew in the Medieval World: A Source Book, 315–1791.* New York: Atheneum, 1969.

MARGOLIS, MAX L., and Marx, Alexander, *A History of the Jewish People.* Philadelphia: Jewish Publication Society, 1927.

MONAS, SIDNEY, *The Third Section, Police and Society in Russia Under Nicholas I.* Cambridge: Harvard University Press, 1961.

PALMER, FRANCIS H. E., *Russian Life in Town and Country.* New York: G. P. Putnam's Sons, 1901.

PAYNE, ROBERT, *The Terrorists.* New York: Funk & Wagnalls, 1957.

PERETZ, I. L., *My Memoirs.* New York: Citadel Press, 1964.

PINSON, KOPPEL S., ed., *Simon Dubnow, Nationalism and History.* Philadelphia: Jewish Publication Society, 1958.

PLOTKIN, ABRAHAM L., *Struggle for Justice.* New York: Exposition Press, 1960.

RAISIN, JACOB S., *The Haskala Movement in Russia.* Westport: Greenwood Press, 1972.

RIBALOW, MENACHEM, *The Flowering of Modern Hebrew Literature.* New York: Twayne, 1959.

ROTH, CECIL, *History of the Jews.* New York: Schocken Books, 1961.

ROTH, CECIL, and Wigodor, Geoffrey, eds., *Encyclopedia Judaica,* 16 vols. Jerusalem: Keter, 1972.

SACHAR, HOWARD M., *The Course of Modern Jewish History.* New York: World Publishing Co., 1958.

SAMUEL, MAURICE, *Prince of the Ghetto.* New York: Schocken Books, 1973.

———, *The World of Sholem Aleichem.* New York: Alfred A. Knopf, 1943.

SCHNEOUR, ZALMAN, *Noah Pandre's Village.* London: Chatto & Windus, 1938.

SCHWARTZ, LEO W., ed., *Great Ages and Ideas of the Jewish People*. New York: Random House, 1956.

SCHWARTZ, SAMUEL, *Tell the Children*. New York: Exposition Press, 1959.

SCHWEITZER, FREDERICK M., *A History of the Jews: Since the First Century A.D.* New York: Macmillan, 1971.

SELZER, MICHAEL, *Wineskin and Wizard*. New York: Macmillan, 1970.

SETON-WATSON, HUGH, *The Russian Empire, 1801–1917*. New York: Oxford, 1967.

SHAZAR, ZALMAN, *Morning Stars*. Philadelphia: Jewish Publication Society, 1967.

SINGER, I. J., *The Brothers Ashkenazi*. New York: Knopf, 1936.

———, *Of a World That Is No More*. New York: Vanguard, 1970.

STEPHENSON, GRAHAM, *Russia from 1812 to 1945*. New York: Praeger, 1970.

STILES, W. C., *Out of Kishinev*. New York: Dillingham, 1903.

THADEN, EDWARD C., *Russia Since 1801*. New York: John Wiley & Sons, 1971.

WAKSMAN, SELMAN, *My Life with the Microbes*. New York: Simon & Schuster, 1954.

WEIZMANN, CHAIM, *Trial and Error: An Autobiography*. Philadelphia: Jewish Publication Society, 1949.

WOLWOLFF, ISRAEL, *I Yield to Destiny*. New York: 1938.

ZBOROWSKI, MARK, and Herzog, Elizabeth. *Life Is with People: The Jewish Little-Town of Eastern Europe*. New York: International Universities Press, 1952.

# Index

267|